Mistress of Our Tears
**A Literary and Bibliographical
Study of Barbara Hofland**

Mistress of Our Tears

A Literary and Bibliographical
Study of Barbara Hofland

Dennis Butts

Scolar Press

© Dennis Butts, 1992

All rights reserved. No part of this publication may be reproduced, stored in a retrieval system, or transmitted in any form or by any means, electronic, mechanical, photocopying, recording, or otherwise without the prior permission of the publisher.

Published by
SCOLAR PRESS
Gower House
Croft Road
Aldershot
Hants GU11 3HR
England

Ashgate Publishing Company
Old Post Road
Brookfield
Vermont 05036
USA

British Library Cataloguing-in-Publication Data is available

ISBN 0 85967 917 9

Camera-ready copy by Sonning Business Services, 6 Glendevon Road, Woodley, Reading, Berks RG5 4PH

Printed in Great Britain by Billing and Sons Limited, Worcester

**For Mary
as always**

Contents

Introduction	1
1 Mrs Hofland, the writer	11
2 Religion, the family, education and work	27
3 Her readers	37
4 Mrs Hofland's books	49
Notes on the arrangement of entries	51
Abbreviations and locations of first and other important editions	52
Abbreviations used in descriptions of the books	55
Chronological listing	56
Editions	96
Contributions to annuals and keepsakes	98

Attributions to Mrs Hofland	99
Dates and locations of contemporary reviews	103
A select bibliography	105
Index of artists, engravers and printers	115
Index of Barbara Hofland's works	117
General index	121

Introduction

In late eighteenth- and early nineteenth-century England, many women began writing for children: Lucy Cameron (1781-1858), Maria Edgeworth (1767-1849), Maria Hack (1777-1844) and Mrs Sherwood (1775-1851), to name some of the most prominent.

Their books tended to be didactic, written in the form of Moral Tales to propagate contemporary moral, social and religious values. But when we examine the works of these writers in detail we often find sharp differences despite apparent similarities. By contrast, Mrs Hofland shows a much greater awareness than her contemporaries of the hard economic facts of life, and her apparently simple stories of domestic life often ask questions about Family, Work and the Role of Women in ways which anticipate the later novels of Dickens, the Brontës and Mrs Gaskell.

The vicissitudes of Mrs Hofland's long, hard, and ultimately heroic life are almost certainly responsible for this. Her life contained triumphs and disasters which she not only drew on for her books, but which also enabled her to develop insights and resolution.

She was born Barbara Wreaks in Sheffield in 1770, the daughter of an ironmonger who died when she was three, leaving his widow to bring up Barbara and a younger boy. Barbara's mother re-married, and Barbara was brought up, evidently happily, by a maiden aunt. To judge from the quotations in her books, she seems to have acquired some kind of education: she was well-acquainted with the Bible, Shakespeare, and most of the English poets, and she had some knowledge of history and geography.

A lively and talented girl, her decorous Augustan verse first appeared in 1794, in the pages of the new Sheffield newspaper *The Iris*. But these were turbulent times, and it is a tribute to Barbara's liberal sympathies and courage that when James Montgomery, the editor of *The Iris*, was imprisoned in 1795 for printing an allegedly seditious ballad, Barbara published a sonnet in praise of his defence lawyer.

At this time Barbara ran her own milliner's shop, but this was sold when she married a prosperous Sheffield businessman, Thomas Hoole, in 1796. A time of great happiness followed, and a baby daughter was born. But tragedy was never far away from Barbara. The child died in 1798 aged fourteen months, and Hoole himself died in March 1799, leaving his young widow to bring up a son aged only four months. To make matters worse, Hoole's business collapsed shortly after his death, and money left to his infant son was also lost when the trustees became insolvent.

Barbara was nothing if not resilient, however. Taking her infant son she went to live with her mother-in-law in nearby Attercliffe, and began to rebuild her shattered world. Throughout her marriage she had continued to write poetry, and encouraged by James Montgomery Barbara collected together her best verses and published them in a volume to be sold by subscription at six shillings a copy. With the help of advertising in *The Iris*, Barbara Hoole's *Poems*, published in 1805, sold over 2,000 copies, 'an event' said the *Gentleman's Magazine* [for a first publication] 'unequalled ..... in the annals of literary history.'

This is pardonable hyperbole, for the remarkable sales figures are perhaps more a tribute to the young widow's personality than to the quality of her poetry; apart from 'Lines occasioned by the death of a little relative', it is disappointing.

With money raised from sales of the poetry Mrs Hoole was able to send her son to a Moravian school and also to open a girls' boarding-school in Harrogate. Encouraged, too, by the success of the poems, she wrote her first children's story, *The History of an Officer's Widow*, in which she told the story of a family and its struggles after the father died of war wounds. John Harris, London's leading publisher of children's books, gave her £6 and published it in 1809, the year in which the school in Harrogate opened.

Other children's books soon followed. Even better was the arrival of a handsome suitor in the person of Thomas Christopher Hofland, a talented but impecunious landscape artist, who met Barbara when poverty forced him to teach art. Though Barbara's friends had reservations about the match, there was no doubt about Hofland's ability - he had exhibited at the Royal Academy since 1798 - and Barbara fell deeply in love with the attractive and engaging artist. They were married in 1810.

At first all went well. Hofland exhibited paintings at the Leeds Art Exhibitions, and his *View of Windermere* was accepted by the Royal Academy. But though Barbara's writing was going well, the school proved a disappointment, not only because of the many difficult pupils but because of their equally difficult parents' reluctance to pay the fees. Even more worrying was the state of Hofland's health. He was ill in January and again in March 1811. Barbara and her husband decided that their problems could best be put behind them by making a fresh start elsewhere. In November 1811 they sold up in Harrogate, and before the year was out had settled in London.

Again all went well initially. Hofland exhibited regularly at the Royal Academy and his picture, 'A Storm off Scarborough' won a prize of 100 guineas awarded by the British Institution. Mrs Hofland's career also prospered. Her moral tale for children, *The Daughter-in-Law*, so impressed Queen Charlotte that she gave Mrs Hofland permission to dedicate *A Visit to London* to herself. And the most popular book, *The Son of a Genius*, published in 1812, reached its tenth edition by 1827. Mrs Hofland was by now well known. She made friends with many celebrities, including the architect John Soane and fellow-writers Maria Edgeworth and Mary Mitford.

In *The Son of a Genius* Mrs Hofland told the story of a talented but imprudent artist who wastes his gifts and almost ruins the lives of his wife and children because of his erratic and unstable temperament. When we read this it is difficult not to suspect that Mrs Hofland was beginning to reflect some of the experiences of her own second marriage. Hofland had been brought up as a leisured gentleman, and despite the fact that he had to earn a living, this is how he still saw himself. He was, for example, frequently away from home, not just on painting expeditions but on fishing jaunts. Then again, although he had successes, these were erratic, perhaps because of his poor health. But although Mrs Hofland's friends had their suspicions, Mrs Hofland never voiced them. The saddest thing of all, however, is that as Hofland's career failed to develop - his tragedy is not unlike that of his friend Benjamin Haydon - so he became extremely difficult to live with, and even, at his worst moments, abused his wife.

Furthermore, in 1816, he produced an illegitimate son, Thomas Richard Hofland, whom his wife took in, nursed, and treated as her own for the rest of her life. Whether it was to avoid embarrassment or for business reasons, the Hoflands moved to Twickenham in the same year, and began work on an important commission for the Marquis of Blandford, heir to the

Duke of Marlborough. The Marquis had bought the mansion of Whiteknights, near Reading, and having spent large sums on its garden and library - paying over £2,000 for a fine edition of *The Decameron*, for example - he engaged the Hoflands to produce a book which would describe his showplace, with illustrations by Hofland to accompany a text written by Barbara. For nearly three years husband and wife worked together on the project, making sketches, employing engravers and printers. But by the time the handsome volume was completed in 1819, although the Marquis had become the Duke of Marlborough, he was virtually bankrupt. The Hoflands received not a penny from him, but they did obtain some return by themselves selling off unwanted copies of the book.

So Hofland's career continued on its erratic way. In 1821 an exhibition of his paintings in New Bond Street was a failure; his outbursts of temper became more noticeable to outsiders. Yet Mrs Hofland continued to support him cheerfully.

'We never heard her utter a complaint or expose any "weakness" of her husband', said a friend.[1]

Children's books continued to flow: *Theodore, or the Crusaders* (1821), *The Daughter of a Genius* (1823), and *William and his Uncle Ben* (1826). *Says She to her Neighbour, What?* was her first adult novel, appearing as early as 1812. More books, some published in three or four volumes, appeared in 1813 and 1814. In the 1820s she produced *Tales of the Manor* for Longmans, but few of her adult novels achieved a second edition, and it is surely significant that when in 1823 the periodical *La Belle Assemblée* published her portrait as a well-known authoress it associated her with *The Son of a Genius* and her other children's books rather than with her adult novels. Her children's books sold all over the world, being particularly popular in America. Her books were also translated into French, Spanish and German.

Mrs. Hofland continued to produce two or three books a year: children's tales, textbooks, essays for the *Annuals*, anything that would bring in money. By the 1830s she often found the physical effort of writing painful because of a shoulder injury but still she kept on writing.

All this time she had been cheered and sustained by the love of her son Frederick, who had gone up to Cambridge had then taken Holy Orders. As a curate in Holborn, he worked unstintingly among the poor; he was one of those Christian priests whose simple goodness shines out amid some of the worst aspects of nineteenth-century England. But in the autumn of 1832 he fell ill, and the mother who had already buried his baby sister and his father now had the task of nursing her son through the last weeks of his life.

Even now she was not finished. There were still books to be written, correspondence with old friends like James Montgomery to keep up, a husband to look after. In 1840 Hofland fulfilled a lifetime's ambition when he visited Italy, but his health continued to deteriorate and on his return in 1843 he died. Despite her loss, Mrs Hofland went on working on her forty-third children's book. She made a last visit to Sheffield where she met again her old friend, James Montgomery.

> 'I have got quite safe to my native town', she wrote to a friend. 'I was tired but a day's quietness restored me, and I am now as well as possible, save my breath; and of that I must not complain. My Heavenly Father deals with me very gently; life has been stormy with me, but I trust my sun will set peacefully.'[2]

She returned home to finish a children's story, *Emily's Reward*, in the summer of 1844, but then an attack of erysipelas was aggravated by a fall - she was now in her 74th year - and she did not have the strength to resist a second attack when it came. She died on 4 November 1844 and was buried in a vault in the parish churchyard, Richmond, Surrey.

Mrs. Hofland is not a major novelist, nor even a major writer of children's books, but her books continue to be of interest, not only because of the courage and attractiveness of the author's personality, but also because they present a remarkably realistic account of everyday life at the beginning of the nineteenth century. They are written from the point of view of a woman of the lower middle-classes, who brings shrewd observation and common-sense to her accounts of family life, of grief and sudden poverty, and of the brave and resourceful ways people, especially women with children, fight to support themselves in decent humane ways.

The Son of a Genius, for example, contrasts the tragedy of Lewis, an artist of genius but unstable temperament, with the story of his young son who supports his mother and sister by selling little drawings in Leeds market for two shillings each, and through virtue and industry finally wins through to the happiness and prosperity which his father's lack of steady application has failed to achieve. The same lesson is repeated in *The History of an Officer's Widow* (1809), *The Blind Farmer and his Children* (1816) and *Alicia and her Aunt* (1822), in each of which Mrs Hofland paints a moving picture of family life and its adversities in ways that later and greater writers followed and developed. *Elizabeth and her Three Beggar Boys* (1833), with its tale of a wandering orphan, points the way forward to Dickens's *Oliver Twist* (1839); while one of Mrs Hofland's very best stories, *Ellen the Teacher* (1814), with its account of a young girl abandoned in a harsh boarding-school who eventually becomes governess in a kinder household, suggests clear links with *Jane Eyre* (1847). (It even has a minor character named Betsey Burns!)

Because Mrs Hofland is an authoress whose talent has been unjustly neglected, research into her life and works has had to take many different paths. For biographical information Thomas Ramsay's mid-Victorian *Life and Literary Remains* (W.J. Cleaver, 1849) must be consulted, but Ramsay seems only to have known Mrs Hofland in the latter part of her life and further details of her life have to be sought from sources as far apart as Iowa and Melbourne, Australia. Details of Mrs Hofland's career as a professional writer are equally elusive. No major library contains a collection of all her published works, and even bibliographical authorities like the *New Cambridge Bibliography of Literature* contain errors and omissions, which the checklist in Chapter 4 now substantially amends. The Longman Archive at Reading University, in particular, has provided a fascinating glimpse of the economics of children's authorship in the 1820s, when Mrs Hofland was published by Longmans for a time.[3]

In the course of my research a great deal of help has been received from many libraries and institutions, usually with a kindness and efficiency, which, though it might be routine for them, it would be foolish to underestimate. Among individuals I am particularly grateful to Brian Alderson (then of the Polytechnic of North London); Professor Marilyn Butler, Cambridge; Drs M. Bott and J.A. Edwards, Reading University; Dr Robert Gittings; Dr Fred Inglis, Warwick University; Mrs Marjorie Moon, Winchester; Dr D. Postles of Sheffield City Library; Eric Quayle, St Ives, Cornwall; Ms Margaret Walters, Reading University; and Dr Shirley Foster of Sheffield University. My greatest thanks are to my wife Mary, not only for her unfailing skill at detecting grammatical errors, but for her Mrs Hofland-like support during all the difficulties encountered when working on the project as a whole.

Dennis Butts

Notes

1 S.C. Hall, *A Book of Memories of Great Men and Women of the Age from Personal Acquaintance*, third edition, London, n.d., p.123.
2 Thomas Ramsay, *The Life and Literary Remains of Barbara Hofland*, London, 1849, p.201.
3 For further details about the life and works of Mrs Hofland, see Dennis Butts, 'Mrs. Barbara Hofland (1770-1844): a biographical and literary study', a thesis submitted for the degree of M.Phil. in the Department of English Literature in the University of Sheffield, 1980.

1 Mrs Hofland, the Writer

Antecedents and contemporaries

> People who need to do good, do not make the characters entirely out of their own heads, Beatrice, but they notice whom they see and know and paint them and their conduct, under circumstances which do, or might, exist in the world, by which means they are enabled to give advice to persons similarly circumstanced - I mean the advice of example.[1]

Mrs. Hofland's books for children relate predominantly to that group of moral, didactic and realistic writers which flourished at the end of the eighteenth and beginning of the nineteenth centuries. The period of change associated with the French Revolution abroad, and the Industrial Revolution at home, through which swirled the cross-currents of Romanticism and Evangelicism, began to produce a greater awareness of the child and of the need to provide him or her with a literature intended to be more serious and sustaining than that deriving from John Newbery and his successors earlier in the century. Instead of verses about games and play, instead of alphabetical rhymes and light-hearted re-tellings of Aesop's *Fables*, we begin to get serious stories of people in real-life situations. Often a young child encounters a dilemma of some kind, perhaps even hardship or death, and has to cope with the crisis, usually with the help of a sympathetic but not necessarily tender-hearted parent or friend, who emphasises the moral or the religious implications of the situation to the child and to the reader.

It is not difficult to identify the writers of this kind, with whom Mrs Hofland had the greatest affinities, and from whom she learned most: Thomas Day, Maria Edgeworth, Hannah More, Mrs Sherwood and Sarah Trimmer.

Thomas Day (1748-89) was an ardent admirer of Rousseau, and tried to put some of the great Frenchman's theories on education into practice in his private life, sometimes with surprising results. He attempted to bring up two young orphan girls following Rousseau's idealised picture of childhood, with a view to providing himself with one as a perfect wife, and though this experiment failed and Day married an heiress, it did not affect his principles, and he actually died from being kicked by a horse which he refused to have strictly disciplined.

Day's book *Sandford and Merton* (begun originally to form part of a compilation with his friend R.L. Edgeworth but actually published separately in three parts in 1783, 1786 and 1789) takes up Rousseau's ideas of education based on guidance and experiment with a wise guardian rather than on compulsory knowledge from a strict authoritarian, and articulates them through the story of a wise clergyman, Dr. Barlow, and two contrasting pupils, Tommy Merton, the spoiled son of a rich sugar-planter, and Harry Sandford, the good-natured son of a plain, honest farmer. Through their small domestic adventures, as when Dr. Barlow denies Tommy a plate of cherries because he refused to do his share of digging the garden, through the use of contrasting moral attitudes embodied in two children, and through the device of having tales within the central tale, Thomas Day achieved great success and exerted an influence on many writers.

Not surprisingly, in view of her father's friendship for Thomas Day, Maria Edgeworth (1767-1849) owes something to him, too, and in *The Parent's Assistant* (1796), *Moral Tales* (1801) and *Harry and Lucy* (1825), she uses such devices as the wise adult, contrasting child-characters, and real-life domestic incidents, as instruments of social and moral education. 'The Good French Governess' (*Moral Tale* No. V), for example, tells how an *émigré* from the French Revolution, Mme Rosier, obtains employment in a somewhat dissipated English household, where she educates Mrs Harcourt's four unruly and spoiled children not only so that they begin to enjoy formal learning, after a visit to 'a rational toyshop', but also more importantly begin to develop morally, so that they become more modest and affectionate compared with some of their affected friends.

Maria Edgeworth is superior to most other writers in this genre, of course, mainly because of the greater richness of her dramatic realism, and this is true even when she was operating within those narrow conventions that were rapidly hardening into stereotypes. In the famous story of 'The Purple Jar', for example, when Rosamund learns the folly of buying a coloured jar which looks attractive but is worthless, instead of something useful like a pair of shoes, she promises to be more sensible next time

> 'I am sure - no, not quite sure,' she tells her mother, 'but I hope I shall be wiser another time,'

and in that child-like hesitation Maria Edgeworth shows her superiority.

Maria Edgeworth is primarily a moral writer, of course, whereas Mrs Hofland is rooted in the Christian tradition of a liberal member of the Church of England. She herself said in a letter to Maria's father:

> In so far as I am a Tale teller, Sir, I am rendered such by the ardent admiration and the deep sense of their utility, with which the unparalleled excellence of Miss Edgeworth's Tales have inspired me .... The necessity of honesty in its most comprehensive sense, has been deeply impressed upon my mind from even infancy, having been a great sufferer from the want of it in others (first as a fatherless child and afterwards as a young widow) but I could never have ventured to display this persuasion if I had not seen how possible it was to render the most simple precepts and homely situations, affecting, improving and delightful, by the stories .... in the Parents (sic) Assistant.

Though not as much influenced by Rousseau as by Thomas Day, Maria Edgeworth's values tend to be based on ethical, practical or social grounds. It is significant, for example, that there is little reference to prayer in her books and few quotations from the Bible. Mrs Trimmer, Hannah More and Mrs Sherwood could not write books without either, and their stories remind us that the Evangelical Revival was contemporaneous with Maria Edgeworth's beginnings and had a wide influence on children's literature for generations.

Mrs Sarah Trimmer (1741-1810) was a firm supporter of the Church of England and an opponent of Rousseauist principles, who became involved in the Sunday School movement in 1782. Her most important book for children, *Fabulous Histories Designed for the Instruction of Children*, was first published in 1786, and achieved enormous popularity under its later title, *The History of the Robins*, which contrasted the lives of a family of robins with the Benson family in whose garden the birds nest. The story is thoroughly didactic; as the young birds learn from their parents not to be extravagant, for example, in the next episode the young Benson children learn not to be cruel to animals. The same combination is also found in Mrs Trimmer's *Instructive Tales*, first found in *The Family Magazine* in 1788-9, although these represent Mrs Trimmer's attempts to bring Christianity into humble homes, and are not specifically for children.

Nor were Hannah More's *Cheap Repository Tracts* (1795-8) addressed directly to children. Nevertheless, by contributing to the religio-literary climate of the age, their influence on children's writers, either directly or indirectly, was enormous. Like Sarah Trimmer, a prominent member of the Sunday School movement, Mrs Hannah More (1745-1833) was asked to write against the Jacobin and atheist literature circulating at the outbreak of war with France, and in a series of brilliant pamphlets, she told simple stories, usually of village life, in which by practising Christian virtues, poor folk found a peace and happiness that no purely political or social changes could hope to provide.

The Evangelical Magazine treated Hannah More's Tracts with some reserve, however, and would have preferred facts instead of fiction, while the founders of the Religious Tract Society regretted that they did not contain a fuller statement of evangelical principles. They regarded the salvation of children as particularly important, and so books preaching the evangelical message for children began to appear, of which those by Mrs Sherwood (1775-1851) were the most remarkable.[2] This is not simply because of her obsession with death in the first part of *The Fairchild Family* (1818), which contains the famous visit to the gibbet in Blackwood, but because in her passionate desire to show how sinful children are and how necessary it is for adults to bring them to salvation, she gives tremendous emphasis to parent-child relationships. Her power and variety in realistically depicting the joys and crises of ordinary life are present as early as *Susan Gray* (1802), and recur throughout her career. In *The Fairchild Family* many children's activities, such as playing with dolls, quarrelling, even over-eating, are evoked against a background of parental assurance and Christian theology.

As well as feeling the immediate influence of other didactic writers of fiction for children, Mrs Hofland's work clearly shares many of the values and attitudes common among almost all writers in the last decades of the eighteenth century. Her sympathies look back to the earlier part of the eighteenth century, as we can see, for instance, by the insistence on the need for judgement and control that is found in some of her book-titles: *Patience and Perseverance* (1813), *Integrity* (1823), *Decision* (1824), *Moderation* (1825), *Reflection* (1826) and *Self-Denial* (1827).

In vocabulary, use of dialogue, and descriptive writing, too, Mrs Hofland belongs very much to the late eighteenth century in range and technique, and especially in that capacity to deal in abstractions and generalisations.

Despite its attempts to hold on to certain Augustan values, however, the late eighteenth century experienced that cult of Sensibility which not only emphasised the freer expression of feelings, especially tears and grief, but saw Sensibility as in some ways conducive to and evidence of moral virtue. J.M.S. Tompkins has shown how the connection between Sensibility and Didacticism probably arose from the way novels tended to be regarded as conduct-books from the time of Richardson onwards, and it is not surprising, therefore, to find young wives prone to tears or heroines to fainting in the works of Mrs Hofland.[3] Maria responds in this way when she learns that the man she loves has put his affection elsewhere:

> 'Love! it was love for you he confessed!' Such were the words that died on Maria's tongue as she sank fainting on the floor in a death-like swoon.[4]

But there was a reaction against excessive feeling by 1798 - we see it in the works of Jane Austen and Maria Edgeworth, of course - and though novelists continued to display Sensibility in their characters, their own values support common sense. And this tends to be Mrs Hofland's position. In a world, as she saw it, full of hardships and poverty and sudden death, compassion was important, but over-indulgence in feelings was a luxury which most people could not afford.

But if it is useful to point to those writers and those areas from which Mrs Hofland may have learned, and with whom she had many similarities, it is also important to insist on the differences in general before going on to try to identify her own individuality more precisely.

Thus, as for the Rousseauists, if we can use that term to describe a group which embraces writers as diverse as Thomas Day, Mary Wollstonecraft and the Edgeworths, while it is clear that Mrs Hofland learned from them in general, and admired Maria Edgeworth in particular, one has to say that in the last resort she is a religious and Christian writer in ways they are not. It is not simply that Mrs Hofland quotes the Bible frequently, though that is extremely important, but that the actions of the characters in her stories are measured against Christian criteria rather than those of reason and social morality.

In her books Mrs Hofland did not shrink from death; she was a realist, after all, who outlived both her husbands, and had buried both her children. But it is not dwelt upon as it is by Mrs Sherwood. Nor did she believe much in physical punishment. The Fairchild children had their hands whipped as well as being taken to Blackwood, but in *Rich Boys and Poor Boys* (1833) when Sophy's father discovers her bad temper, he does not punish her but urges her to learn self-control, and her brothers and sisters promise to help her.

It was perhaps to the tracts of Hannah More that Mrs Hofland owed most, but even here important distinctions have to be made. Mrs Hofland's moral tales were written for children, not for poor adults; they are stories, not tracts. Relying more on realistic accounts of an urban and industrial society than Hannah More's agrarian fables, Mrs Hofland's values are those of a liberal member of the Church of England who follows the ethics of the Sermon on the Mount without too much heart-searching, while Hannah More puts more emphasis on a sense of sin, and the need for penitence and grace. Thus while Mrs Hofland's story, *The Blind Farmer*, is not unlike *The Shepherd of Salisbury Plain* by Hannah More in some ways, both narrative and social milieu are much more fully developed, and when the farmer is ejected from his farm he goes to Birmingham, and to regain their lost prosperity, his children find work in factories.

Mrs Hofland's individuality

What is there about Mrs Hofland's work that gave it a popularity in her day, and kept her in print until almost the very end of the Victorian Age?

An examination of *The Son of a Genius* (1812) seems a good place to start. The fourth of her stories for children, it became the most popular of all her books, reached its fourteenth edition by 1841, and remained in print long after that, earning the praise of R.L. Edgeworth, and favourable comments from Lady Eastlake - 'a very beautiful tale' she called it - and as late as 1894 from Alfonzo Gardiner.

The theme of the book is partly responsible, for in introducing this tale of the vicissitudes of a poor artist's wife and family, Mrs Hofland declares her major aim was to show that

> 'the most brilliant talents, enlarged conceptions, and refined sensibilities, of which human nature is capable, may be rendered useless, and even prejudicial, unless they are directed by prudence, humility and discretion; and above all, that strict integrity, founded on religious principles' (pp. iv-v).

The narrative is thus firmly structured from the beginning to articulate a particular set of Christian and moral attitudes, and does so through the story of the unhappy life and struggles of

Lewis, the artist of genius, his long-suffering wife Agnes, and their son Ludovico. And it is of this kind of story that Mary Mitford was presumably thinking when she told Mrs Hofland

'You are the mistress of our tears, as Miss Austen is of our smiles, and,' she goes on, 'I think you have an advantage.'[5]

Yet, though the book is written from the standpoint of an omniscient Christian author offering a moral commentary on her narrative to her young readers, it is not without dramatic detail or scenes. Physical description of character is rare, but the story proceeds by a mixture of short scenes, in which dialogue is quite prominent, with much reported or summarised action.

The number of detailed references to money in the tale is quite extraordinary, from the details of the artist's debts to the exact cost of his son's apprenticeship.[6]

That Mrs Hofland's concern with money matters is partly due to the circumstances of her own life cannot be doubted. Widowed at an early age, the discovery that her late husband's business had foundered, then the long years of supporting her second husband's unsuccessful artistic career, could not help but make her aware of the importance of money. When she writes about working in a milliner's shop, being a teacher, or selling pictures, she speaks with a rare authority, and this gives her books a particular interest.

Indeed, she is almost a classic example of those women who, in what Ellen Moers has called the Epic Age of Women's Literature, turned to writing in order to earn, and in doing so wrote about money, work, and the crucial importance of financial independence with such realism because their fates, if single or widowed, were even more financially determined than those of men.

It is clear, too, that Mrs Hofland sees or wishes her readers to see some kind of relationship between what she regarded as the upholding of Christian virtues, trust in God, patience, charity realism, moderation, self-control, and their reward, not simply in spiritual blessings but on this earth now.

The particular interest of Mrs Hofland's tales lies very often in the way she shows us people, frequently children or adolescents, struggling in adverse circumstances to maintain some kind of integrity and Christian virtue, and at the same time exercising all kinds of industry and business acumen to support themselves and their families. And it is part of her belief that this combination of qualities is related in some way, and though tested out in many trying circumstances is nearly always rewarded.

Mrs Hofland's belief in the necessity of certain values and her optimism about their material reward was not new, of course. It appears in some of Hannah More's *Cheap Repository Tracts*, and Gillian Avery, among others, has pointed to the simple materialism of many children's books from 1770 onwards.[7] But what is new in Mrs Hofland's work is the greater realism of detail and complexity with which she handles this kind of material in a much more achieved, more sophisticated fiction, and which she relates or seeks to relate to a whole system of Christian values in a more industrialised urban society. In her books there is more about budgeting than mad dogs, and the pressures of debt and bankruptcy are never far away.

Mrs Hofland was not a Puritan, but she was sympathetic to that unconscious system of beliefs which between the sixteenth and nineteenth centuries saw a relationship between religious faith, the need to practise certain rules of conduct, and their economic consequences, and then tended to use the economic consequences as evidence of that religious belief and practice. Because of this it is tempting to argue that there is a contradiction in Mrs Hofland's tales between her interest in work and money, and her profession of Christianity; it is as if she were only interested in financial matters but felt the need to pay lip service to a rather more overtly respectable moral creed. But to do so would be a mistake. Mrs Hofland's primary values are Christian, of a broadly ethical rather than a strictly doctrinal kind perhaps, with an emphasis on faith in God, patience, honesty, compassion and industry, virtues which she believed, perhaps a little naively, tended to lead to economic survival and even prosperity. She does not make the mistake of identifying wealthy people automatically with recipients of grace, nor does she ever advocate actions leading to economic rewards which are in conflict with Christianity. In her work there is no trace of Pecksniff's hypocrisy, nor is there that tension between money-making and the confession of sin which characterises Defoe's *Moll Flanders*. Her heroes and heroines are good, honest, compassionate beings, whose virtue is rewarded in this world as well as the next, like the characters in Fielding, Jane Austen and Dickens.

But Mrs Hofland does just a little more than articulate some of the main features of the Protestant ethic of the time, and though her way of doing so was perhaps unconscious, and is often embarrassingly clumsy, it does make her values clearer, and can sometimes be moving.

There is a providential element about some of the coincidences, often a clumsy feature of Mrs Hofland's tales, but which can occasionally achieve a moving effect by being linked morally to earlier events in their stories. For example, in *The Son of a Genius*, when Ludovico tries to refuse a reward for returning a lost bank-note, his mother reassures him with the following words:

> 'Take it, my love, by all means, since Mr Higgins has the goodness to give it to you, and consider it not only as his gift, but that of a gracious Providence who has given you another friend in the hour of need, remembering also, that although this appears an accidental good, yet it came to you in the prosecution of a regular system of industry, which is ever beneficial.' (p. 129).

There are coincidences and coincidences, in other words, and some are based on divine recognition of worth and justice. In *Ellen the Teacher*, quite late in the story Ellen's brother, Tom, rescues an old lady from a coach accident, and she turns out to be their grandmother who had treated their mother so harshly when, in the first chapter, she married against her wishes. Now the grandmother is overcome with remorse for this ill-treatment and makes up for it with generous financial settlements.

Similarly, in *The Blind Farmer*, Sir Harry Eustace gives money for a blind farmer to have an expensive eye-operation, not knowing it is the same man he had foolishly evicted at the start of the tale. Later in the story he helps the farmer's son in his career as an artist, again unaware of the moral connections between them. But Mrs Hofland and the reader are aware, and if Mrs Hofland seems to stretch the long arm of coincidence too far at times, using the device crudely or sentimentally, there is something clumsily moving about her belief that Providence does look after ill-treated grandchildren and evicted tenants who have lived good lives. 'Even matters of chance seem most marvellous,' says Aristotle, 'if there is an appearance of design as it were in them', and many of Mrs Hofland's apparent coincidences seem to fit into her moral pattern.

When we begin to consider Mrs Hofland's literary techniques more formally, perhaps the most important feature to emphasise is that in many ways she is a transitional writer. While possessing many of the characteristics of eighteenth-century prose writers, she looked forward in terms of realistic texture towards the great nineteenth-century novelists. Her work is often half-generalised in terms of characterisation, descriptive writing, and fable-like plots, but also half-enmeshed in the details of everyday family and business life in northern industrial towns.

As the wife of an artist, she naturally pays a good deal of attention to landscape, though it is often described in vague, generalised terms.

But although one may regret that Mrs Hofland's descriptive

writing lacks the acutely selected detail of Jane Austen, for example, within the conventions of the moral tale she is able to depict people's reactions to scenery quite sharply. Emily, in *The Sisters* (1866), goes to visit some country cottages, knowing all about their picturesque qualities, but when she actually enters a poor man's house, reality is quite different:

> Emily shuddered. 'Is this', said she, 'the interior of a cottage? I thought the people were ruddy laughing rustics; but this poor man is sick and ill, just as I have been; but alas! how differently situated!' (pp. 69-70).

The same mixture of abstraction and particularity is also found in the way Mrs Hofland depicts people. As a moralist working to demonstrate the superiority of one set of values over another, she very often articulates these differences through contrasting characters, with one person or group representing the approved values and another person or group representing their opposites. In *Moderation*, worldly Harriet and fanatical Sophia are compared with their sister Emma and found wanting, while in *The Daughter of a Genius* the contrast is between the foolish mother and her more balanced daughter.

There is, then, often a schematic and static element present in the books, with characters representing certain values and behaviour in predictable ways in order to illustrate them. But Mrs Hofland is also able to suggest complexity at times, and even show characters developing, as Clara does in *Reflection*.

The pathos Mrs Hofland evokes from death-scenes is often extremely limited and is unlikely to have much effect on modern readers. For though death abounds in her books, obviously in those about widowhood, but also in others - *The Son of a Genius* and *The Daughter-in-Law* - where young children die, one's unease is not about historical accuracy, but about the literary presentation, with its heavy reliance on prolix and formal rhetoric and the stylised gesture of the dying person. The unsuccessful artist's death in *The Son of a Genius* rings particularly false.

Mrs Hofland sometimes had difficulties dealing with the framework of a full-length novel, and this partly explains their unsatisfactory quality. In the early nineteenth century a full-length novel meant one of three or four Volumes, of course, and Mrs Hofland tried to extend the length by such devices as spreading a family history over several generations, by the labyrinthine use of subplots, by tales within tales, by scholarly notes - as in the historical romance *The King's Son* - or by frankly admitting that her story will not stretch to three volumes and, to avoid giving short measure, adding a second story.[8]

Happily the shorter length and often schematic form of the moral tale, with its reliance on contrasting scenes of good and bad behaviour, gave her fewer difficulties. She was able to link domestic episodes together neatly and to illustrate the values she was endorsing with realistic and well-chosen incidents in ways that appealed to children, and her adventure stories like *The Stolen Boy* and *The Young Crusoe* were deservedly popular.

The main impulse for much of Mrs Hofland's work was autobiographical. A widow herself, she wrote three tales about widows, even discussing the deceptive nature of the consumption which killed her first husband.[9] Married to one, and friendly with other impoverished artists, she wrote about them and their struggle to survive. Her work as a milliner and a teacher found a place in her tales, and she even introduces real people like John Soane, as well as references to her own husband.[10] Obviously she felt that the connection between fiction and real life was important, partly because it suited her temperament, and partly, one suspects, because of the lingering public feeling that novel-reading was a source of corruption.

Despite her researches, however, the second-hand experience of her travel-stories gives them a faded quality. Even the moral tales are often flawed by the conventional views of the genre cutting across the small but personal view Mrs Hofland was able to communicate. She could not handle a large canvas, and carelessness and prolixity, induced almost certainly by the economic need to produce work quickly, weakened the directness of even her short tales.

It was, however, only one among the many misfortunes of her life that Mrs Hofland was never able to give her books the care and revision they required. That she persisted in writing was mainly for economic reasons, of course, but there was something poignantly courageous about the way she continued writing until well into her seventies.

And her literary strengths are related to her courage, for they are local and embodied best in those scenes where ordinary human beings pull themselves together and demonstrate their strengths after some great domestic grief or crisis. We see it when Mrs Daventry's young family rally round their mother after their father's death and financial ruin in *The Merchant's Widow*, and when the Blind Farmer's family, evicted from their farm, settle at Birmingham and begin work again.

'In this manner, by unremitting industry, though with very small profits, the distressed family made shift to support themselves',

says Mrs Hofland[11], and if that call to labour and endurance reminds us of later children's writers like Mrs Molesworth and Mrs Nesbit, the comparison is not wholly to Mrs Hofland's disadvantage.

Notes

1 Mrs Hofland, *The Godmother's Tales*, London, 1842, p.69.
2 For fuller accounts of this complicated movement with particular reference to children and education, see Paul Sangster, *Pity My Simplicity*, London, 1963, and also M. Nancy Cutt, *Mrs Sherwood and her Books for Children*, Oxford, 1974.
3 J.M.S. Tompkins, *The Popular Novel in England 1770-1800*, London, 1932 (Chapter III). Though Dr Tompkins' argument refers mainly to adult novels, it applies equally well to children's books.

4 *Decision*, 'A New Edition', London, 1840, p.86.
5 Mary Mitford to Mrs Hofland, 17 April 1819; see Henry Chorley, *Letters of Mary Russell Mitford*, Second Series, two vols, London, 1872, I, p.69.
6 See pages 21,28,33,47,51,58,79,107,108,119,151,172-3,191,222,232-49.
7 G. Avery, *Childhood's Pattern*, London, 1975, p.(24).
8 A device she used in both *The Captives in India*; and *A Widow and a Will* (3 vols), 1834; and *Daniel Dennison and the Cumberland Statesman* (3 vols), 1846.
9 See *The Daughter-in-Law* and *Says She to her Neighbour, What?*
10 See *The History of a Merchant's Widow and her Young Family*, "New Edition", London, n.d., pp. 54-57.
11 *The Blind Farmer*, 6th edition, London, n.d., pp. 39-40.

2 Religion, the Family, Education and Work

The great concerns of Mrs Hofland's life and writings are Religion, the Family, Education and Work.

If we begin by considering Mrs Hofland's religious views, it is useful to remind ourselves of the biographical facts. She was baptised, married and buried in the Church of England, and her only son was an ordained priest who died a curate in one of London's poorer parishes. Her life and books are thus complementary; there is no clash between the Christian faith she practised in her daily life and what she preached in her books.

But it is important to emphasise that Mrs Hofland was not a religious writer who used fiction as a way of discussing theological issues. Nor does she write about loss of faith. In writing her stories of domestic crises and triumphs, rather than commenting on specific theological issues Mrs Hofland's tales assume a background of Christian faith, which she then uses as the criteria by which to judge her characters and their actions.

Her own religious values are those of a moderate liberal member of the Church of England, untroubled by doubt, confident of Christ's salvation, and striving to practice the teaching of the New Testament, with an emphasis on love, honesty, truthfulness and prudence.

Most of Mrs Hofland's stories deal with family life, and reflect many of the characteristics of the Modern Family that had appeared in much of middle-class England by the beginning of the nineteenth century. Though grandparents, unmarried relatives and even adopted members formed part of some groups, the normal family was much more likely to be restricted to parents and children only. The general contemporary attitudes towards family life were that it was bound together by strong ties of affection, with people marrying for love rather than for economic reasons, parents devoting a good deal of time and energy to the upbringing of their children, and children returning this affection with trust and loyalty. Mrs Hofland's work reflects most of these attitudes.

In many of her stories marriage is based upon love - and where it is not, Mrs Hofland is critical. A wedding is usually preceded by a courtship during which the lovers need to explore their feelings towards each other and to satisfy themselves that their love is supported by other considerations. For example, in *Self-Denial* Caroline falls romantically in love with her rich and handsome cousin Charles Ravensworth. 'His cheerful voice .... seemed to diffuse joy through the house the moment he entered it', we are told, and Mrs Hofland adds that 'Like every other young woman, Caroline had formed in her own mind a *beau ideal* of the lover to whom she could surrender her whole heart'.[1] But he turns out to be inconsistent, unreliable, and a gambler, and after his death Caroline begins to find pleasure in the company of Sir Mervyn, where 'a silent yet clear understanding of the feelings of each other seemed for a few moments, to pervade and feed the hearts of each' (p. 212).

Clearly considerations of mutual respect and prudence play an important part in choosing a spouse. Excessive passion and premarital sex are totally disapproved of, and though Mrs Hofland cannot deal with these themes in her children's books - as she does in her adult novel, *The Unloved One* - she can and does disapprove very strongly of secret engagements and elopements.

Once the wedding has taken place, Mrs Hofland's ideal of married life is one where husband and wife in conditions of mutual love and support create a harmonious environment for their children to grow up in. This is perhaps best realized in *The Blind Farmer*. But Mrs Hofland is not afraid to suggest that unalloyed bliss does not always follow, and she deals quite openly with difficulties arising within marriage - due to unstable husbands in *The Son of a Genius*, or foolishly romantic wives as in *The Daughter of a Genius*.

The task of bringing up the children is usually shared, with the wife tending to defer to the husband on moral matters, but herself taking more responsibility for the academic learning. The generally expressed attitudes of wives and mothers are always of subordinate and unswerving support for their husbands in almost all matters, even when they are as unreliable as Mr Lewis in *The Son of a Genius*.

However, while generally accepting the principle of wifely subordination, just once or twice Mrs Hofland shows how it can lead to tensions within marriage by way of suppressed feelings. For example, what emerges clearly in several stories is the revelation that some wives have strengths unsuspected by their husbands. In *The Merchant's Widow*, when Mr Daventry dies Mrs Daventry manages very capably and, we are told, he

> 'had never seen the superior mind of his excellent lady'[2] ... 'In fact, he considered her as more dependent upon him than she really was, for Mrs Daventry was not only an accomplished, elegant woman, but (notwithstanding ... the gentle timidity which marked her conduct as a wife) she possessed a strong mind, an

enlightened understanding, and that sense of power which is derived from the constant exercise of religious principles' (p.3).

A similar point is made in *Ellen the Teacher* when Mrs Delville finds that she can manage business affairs better than her husband, but has to conceal the fact to avoid hurting his feelings. The most touching picture of the wife who has to be careful, however, is in *The Son of a Genius*, for when Mrs Lewis's artist husband fails to support the family his wife has to set to and earn a living by making gloves to sell - secretly, to avoid hurting her husband's pride.

With insights into marriage which take account of the social situation but also show a sensitive regard for husbands and wives as troubled human beings, Mrs Hofland is almost a very good writer. But the insights are never sustained dramatically for very long, and what remains is the reader's feeling that although committed to the ideal of marriage, Mrs Hofland believed that at least some wives had the ability to play a larger part in marriage than did many of her contemporaries.

In Mrs Hofland's books part of the wife's normal role is to act with the husband as moral guardian of the children, seeing that they grow up to be good as well as knowledgeable. Her earthly reward is to see them grow up healthy and virtuous, but also, if possible, prosperous and respectable.

The children in Mrs Hofland's books are often less vividly realised than their parents. The girls are nearly always religious and graceful, while the boys are courteous and responsible, with the physical appearance of both conveyed only in the most general terms. A certain amount of writing to formula is visible in the way the boys seem to be of either a manly or a scholarly disposition, a combination frequently found within the same family, and a formula similar to that used for the boys is found in the way Mrs Hofland often characterises her girls: a prudent heroine is often contrasted with one of vitality or even foolishness - as Emma is contrasted with Harriet and Sophia in

Moderation.

Mrs Hofland was not simply interested in the behaviour of children within the family, however. As a mother, a one-time teacher, and a children's writer, she had a natural interest in children's education.

Schoolbooks at the beginning of the nineteenth century tended to be written in the dialogue form of questions and answers - what has been called 'catechetical'. [3]

Though Mrs Hofland produced two textbooks similar to this genre in *The Panorama of Europe* (1813) and *Africa Described* (1828), some idea of a rather more interesting way Mrs Hofland believed children could be stimulated to learn is suggested by her books *Theodore* and *Adelaide*, where history is combined with adventure, and in her travel stories where she tries to make geography come alive by describing a boy's visits to India and the Holy Land.

When she writes about girls' boarding-schools Mrs Hofland's authority is most apparent, and she writes with real conviction. With *Ellen the Teacher* especially, first published as early as 1814, she helped to establish the genre of the governess-novel, and the book achieved great popularity, going into nine editions by 1841, and still in print in the latter part of the century.

In many ways it is a typical Hofland story: a young person achieves victory over poverty and misfortune and ends up successful and prosperous. But at the same time, it paints a graphic and moving picture of school life for many children at the beginning of the nineteenth century. The book's influence on Charlotte Brontë may have been considerable, for it has many parallels with *Jane Eyre*.

The library of the Keighley Mechanics Institute, where the Revd Patrick Brontë and his daughters borrowed books, contained thirty stories by Mrs Hofland.

Discussion of the experiences of Alicia and Ellen as teachers is a reminder of how much attention is given to paid employment generally in Mrs Hofland's stories. The fact that nearly all her characters have a job and that there is an almost endless curiosity about what people do for a living give her books a realism missing from the work of most earlier writers.

Clergymen, teachers and governesses are fairly common, as we have seen, and it is not surprising that Mrs Hofland also described the working lives of artists or boys who made a career in the army or navy. But she also describes people working as brickmakers and potters in *Elizabeth and her Three Beggar Boys*, as silver platers in *The Good Grandmother*, becoming apothecaries and milliners in *The Clergyman's Widow*, wholesale merchants in *The Affectionate Brothers*, interpreters in *William and his Uncle Ben*, or working at home glove-making in *The Son of a Genius*.

Despite this apparent breadth, it is important not to claim too much for Mrs Hofland. These occupations were predominantly of the kind middle-class people turned to in distressed circumstances. Surprisingly, Mrs Hofland has nothing to say about the textile industry where women predominated, and very little about domestic service. Indeed, even when she does write about work, the amount of hard detail she conveys can vary enormously. What she has to say about earnings is usually more specific. Despite all these reservations, Mrs Hofland's treatment of work is still considerable, especially when compared with that of her contemporaries, notably Jane Austen.

About boys' work she makes two minor but interesting points, clearly related to the social and economic conditions of the early nineteenth century. First she stresses how fortunate people are who have work of their own choice, and she reminds her readers of the importance of doing their best in whatever occupation they find themselves. *The Officer's Widow* is virtually written to endorse this theme, for Charles, who wants to be a clergyman, has to make his career in the army, while his brother Henry who actually wanted to be a soldier is obliged to become a linen-draper instead. Yet both have opportunities to show their virtues, and the moral of this tale is that while parents and children should follow their chosen careers if they can, 'in every station in life, a man may find occasion to display those virtues he does possess and acquire those in which he is deficient' (p.170).

It is, however, when she writes of woman and work that Mrs Hofland writes with real conviction and no little originality. As we have seen, she is a firm advocate of love, marriage and family life, and indeed some of her most touching moments arise when she depicts the love and co-operation between members of a family at a time of crisis - the death of a parent or a great financial crash.

In a number of stories, however, harassed wives or widows reveal strength and ability at a time of crisis, and this strength is practical as well as moral. In *The Son of a Genius* Mrs Lewis helps to support her family when her unsuccessful artist husband fails to do so; and in *The Merchant's Widow* Mrs Daventry, underestimated by her husband in his lifetime, begins to reveal her strengths as she recovers from her grief.

Considering both the social situation at the time and the circumstances of her own second marriage, it is clear and perhaps not very surprising that Mrs Hofland could both see sharply and at times feel strongly about the neglect of women's talents. Deeply committed to marriage and the role of the wife as home-maker, when Mrs Hofland writes about women and work she cannot help showing at times what Patricia Thomson has called 'the insidious percolation, often against the author's will, of the new ideas that were beginning to undermine the Victorian domestic idyll.'[4]

In revealing the virtues of some of her heroines, often in contrast with their less able husbands, she was inadvertently suggesting other or complementary roles. In most situations it needed either widowhood or an economic crisis of some kind for that role to be discovered, but as Mrs Hofland goes on to show, society only offered women of her class three kinds of work.

Few of Mrs Hofland's characters become servants, perhaps because such work was outside her own experience. Mrs Thornton's maid Betsey in *Elizabeth and her Three Beggar Boys* is almost the only example and she is working-class. But Mrs Hofland knew very well the problems of governesses and teachers, as we have seen in such stories as *Alicia and her Aunt* and *Ellen the Teacher*.

Her descriptions of millinery and lace-making and glove-making show a similar command of the nature of the work. Mary in *The Good Grandmother*, for example, makes caps and broad-hems shirt ruffles and cravats, before being taken on as a milliner's apprentice, eventually finishing by marrying the manager of the shop. Mrs Ideson in *The Clergyman's Widow*, on the other hand, charges Maria twenty guineas for her apprenticeship, and when she realises that Maria's mother will have difficulties in finding this sum, she helps her to raise it by paying her to make linen gloves at home. When Maria does well she leaves Mrs Ideson and sets up on her own as a chamber-milliner.

In the most remarkable of her books which deal with the question of women and work, Mrs Hofland comes near to writing a feminist novel. *Decision* demonstrates the need for moral firmness and self-control, and this is articulated through what looks like Mrs Hofland's familiar mode: a family's economic distress and then their recovery to a happy ending.

When Maria learns that her father has squandered his wife's fortune as well as his own, she decides that the remaining money and property must be used to repay their outstanding debts, and then, astonishingly, with six pounds borrowed from a friend, the nineteen year-old girl declares her intention of becoming an iron-merchant!

Despite the roughness of the work and the genteel protests

of parents and friends, Maria prospers because, through the sale of steel to the poorer artisans, she is meeting a real need.

It is significant that Maria continues in business after she could have sold the concern and returned to her former way of life, and that though disappointed in one love affair she does in fact turn down two proposals of marriage. The reader familiar with Mrs Hofland's other tales confidently expects her to marry the amiable German she meets through business, and when she declines him, to accept the hand of her first love who returns to her a widower; but in fact she declines both offers, preferring instead to go on living with her aged mother.

The truth is that Maria is an early example of the career-woman, married to her job, to use the well-worn phrase, and that though Mrs Hofland would have denied it, *Decision* is almost a subversive book.

One has to admit that such writing is not common, however, and that although Mrs Hofland followed her own line on Religion, Education and Work, she did so with moderation, and within broad areas of agreement with her contemporaries. Her liberal and broadly ethical interpretation of Christianity, her relaxed attitudes about the upbringing of children, and her probably unconscious advocacy of more fulfilling work for women, even her own blend of eighteenth-century tract style with nineteenth-century realism, give her an individuality which helps to disturb our stereotyped view of the literature of the time, but it would be wrong to think of her as genuinely radical. A Christian, who asserted the importance of marriage and family life as supremely fulfilling for most adults, and wished to teach her children to grow up in the same world of work and worship and love, she was shrewd enough to see and to reflect in her books what was happening around her, even if her instincts were usually conservative. 'She [Mrs Hofland] is womanly to her fingers' ends, and as truthful and independent as a skylark' to quote Mary Mitford, and it is not a bad judgment.[5]

Notes

1 *Self-Denial*, 'New Edition', London, 1846, pp.48-9.
2 *The History of a Merchant's Widow and her Young Family*, 'New Edition', London, n.d., p.7.
3 F.J. Harvey Darton, *Children's Books in England*, third edition, 1982, Cambridge, p.48.
4 Patricia Thomson, *The Victorian Heroine*, Oxford, 1957, p.7.
5 Mary Mitford to Sir William Elford, 30 September 1820, *The Life of Mary Russell Mitford* related in a selection from her friends, edited by the Revd A.G. L'Estrange, 3 vols, London, 1870, II, p.111.

3   Her Readers

Though Mrs Hofland's works are little known today she was a popular author in the nineteenth century, and it is worth examining the appeal of her books in some detail.

The publishing history of her writings can be traced from earliest beginnings at the end of the eighteenth century in Sheffield, and though the records are sometimes incomplete, it is possible to build up a picture of her readership and also to throw some light on what it meant to be an author of children's books in a relatively inaccessible literary period. By looking at what contemporaries said in their reviews and periodicals, moreover, we can obtain some idea of what her readers thought of her books, what they looked for, what they admired, and what they disliked.

Mrs Hofland's literary career began before her first marriage, when a handful of her poems were published in the pages of Montgomery's weekly newspaper, *The Iris*, so the creative impulse was present before widowhood and economic distress forced her to consider the financial rewards of authorship. The death of her first husband and his business losses compelled her to consider writing as a way of earning money, however, and helped by Montgomery she published her first book, *Poems*, in 1805.

Her career as an author made further headway in the next few years, during which she set up a school in Harrogate, met and married her second husband, and then moved to London at the end of 1811. She produced three more books of verse in Yorkshire; the juvenile *La Fête de la Rose* (1809), which had reached a third edition by 1810, *Tales, in Verse* in 1810, and *A Season at Harrogate* (1812). More importantly, however, she succeeded in establishing contact with two of the leading London publishers, John Harris who published her first tale, *The Officer's Widow* in 1809, and Longman, which published her *Little Dramas* in 1810.

Even more success was to follow. Through her contact with the Minerva Press, first made famous under William Lane, the publisher of Gothic novels, Mrs Hofland began to have her adult novels published. The popularity of these novels, and indeed Mrs Hofland's later books for adults, is doubtful, however. R.D. Altick has calculated that novels such as these, in three or four volumes and intended for circulating libraries, usually had a first edition of about 1,000-1,250 copies, and *A Father as he should be* was the only one of Mrs Hofland's to reach a second edition in her lifetime.[1] We cannot be quite sure what these books earned their author, though Dorothy Blakey estimates that most Minerva Press authors received about thirty pounds a book,[2] and this seems to be confirmed in a letter from Mrs Hofland to R.L. Edgeworth; 'for my Patience & Perseverance in 4 Vols I received 30£ in two payments at six months, my "Says She to her neighbour".... procured me 40£.'[3]

In addition to circulating-library novels, however, Lane had always published a few fairy tales and books for the young, and when he was succeeded by a former apprentice, A.K. Newman in 1809, this policy was extended. Furthermore, Mrs Hofland continued to work for Newman when he abandoned the imprint of the Minerva Press and began to publish under his own name. Additionally, in the 1830s he acquired a number of Mrs Hofland's books which had been published initially by Longman, and reprinted them under his own name; Mrs Hofland was still writing for him as late as 1842, when he published *The Godmother's Tales*. Though we do not know the size of Newman's editions - they might have been as small as the 500 copies Longman occasionally printed - an edition of 1,000-2,000 seems more likely, partly because, as the numbers of reprints and reviews show, these titles were evidently popular, and partly because Newman must have found it profitable to continue publishing Mrs Hofland's works for so many years.[4]

Mrs Hofland's second important publisher was John Harris, the famous publisher of children's books, and successor to Elizabeth Newbery of St Paul's Churchyard. He had already published *The Officer's Widow*, and the fact that he did not publish another book of hers till 1812 suggests that Mrs Hofland was dissatisfied with his terms. Indeed she told R.L. Edgeworth that 'My Officer's Widow now in its 4th Edition was sold to Mr Harris for only 6£ nor did he give me a single copy so that asking ten for the "Son of a Genius", was a bold thing'.[5] Despite Marjorie Moon's researches there is no precise knowledge of the size of Harris's editions, but it is unlikely they were smaller than those of other publishers;[6] books were very frequently reprinted, whether Harris's rates of pay were good or not. *The Son of a Genius* reached a 14th edition by 1841, *Ellen the Teacher* was printed at least nine times by the same date, and *The Blind Farmer* achieved seven editions by 1831. Mrs Hofland stayed with John Harris and then his son for many years. Her last book, *Emily's Reward*, was published by their successors, Grant and Griffith, in 1844.

Mrs Hofland's third major publisher was Longman, and here

through the survival of the firm's records[7] it is possible to have a much more precise picture of Mrs Hofland's readership, though it is important to remember that her main dealings with Longman were in the 1820s, by which time her popularity had begun to wane. She first seems to have had dealings with them when they sold copies of *La Fête de la Rose* on a commission basis; they also published an edition of 750 copies of her *Little Dramas* in 1810. Two other titles - *A Season at Harrogate* (1812) and *The Sisters* (1813) were probably also sold by Longman on a commission basis.

Longman's main relationship with Mrs Hofland seems to have developed in the 1820s, however, when they published three adult novels - *Tales of the Priory* (1820), *Tales of the Manor* (1821) and *Beatrice* (1829) - a textbook *Africa Described* (1828), and no fewer than six of her children's tales. The Longman Archives show that 750 copies of *Tales of the Priory* were printed, and 500 each of the other two novels. None merited a second edition, so that it seems safe to say that they failed to achieve much popularity. The textbook was published in an edition of 1,000 copies, and a second edition in 1834.

The children's tales, on the other hand - *Integrity* (1823), *Decision* (1824), *Patience* (1824), *Moderation* (1825), *Reflection* (1826) and *Self-Denial* (1827) - were published initially in editions of 1,000 copies and were reprinted fairly quickly. *Decision* and *Patience* both reached four editions, *Integrity* a third, and the last three second editions - *Self-Denial*, 250 copies and *Reflection*, 249 copies. Mrs Hofland's popularity was clearly diminishing by the late 1820s, and Longmans sold off copies to Newman in June 1833.

Longman seem to have paid Mrs Hofland £25 for the copyright of the first edition. For subsequent editions, however, Longman shared the profits equally with the authoress after they had paid off the cost of reprinting. Thus on second and subsequent editions of *Integrity*, first published in 1823, but reprinted in 1824 and 1826 - a reasonably popular book in other words - Mrs Hofland's annual earnings were as follows: 1825: £7 11s. 10d.; 1826: £15 14s. 5d.; 1827: £9 15s. 9d.; 1830: £2 4s. 1d.; 1831: £5 17s. 11d.; 1832: £2 19s. 6d.; and 1833: £2 19s. 8d.

These payments, which are broadly similar to the sums that Mrs Hofland received for other books at the time,[8] make it clear that she could never have earned much from her writing. Maria Edgeworth's earnings were greater, and an enormously popular adult novelist like Charlotte Smith might obtain at least £75 for a book of juvenile poems in 1804, but their earnings were probably quite exceptional.[9]

It is not surprising that Mrs Hofland continued writing through the 1830s, mainly for A.K. Newman; she even managed to produce three adult novels for Henry Colburn and one for Richard Bentley. But these did not enjoy the reprintings of her children's books.

Mrs Hofland was also able to supplement her income with stories and poems in the *Annuals* and *Pocket Books* - Rudolph Ackermann's *Forget-Me-Not* for instance - which were very popular at the time,[10] and which probably earned her the £5 which Mary Mitford offered to a contributor to *Finden's Tableaux* in 1837.[11]

Despite these poor rewards there can be no doubt that Mrs Hofland was a popular author, widely read overseas as well as in England. Maria Edgeworth wrote home from France in July 1820 to say how well *The Son of a Genius*, under the title of *Ludovico*, had been translated into French,[12] and Mrs Hofland herself claimed that the book had been translated 'into every European language; and in France, Germany and Holland gone through numerous editions.'[13] The Catalogue of the Bibliothèque Nationale records no fewer than nine French editions of *The Stolen Boy*, for example; there was also a German edition.[14]

In America Mrs Hofland was even more popular. *The Son of a Genius* was published in New York as early as 1814, and *Ellen* the Teacher, The Officer's Widow, and Says She to her Neighbour, What? followed a year later. The National Union Catalogue records no fewer than 112 different American editions of her books, as well as several composite volumes containing two or more tales.

In 1849 Ramsay calculated that nearly 300,000 copies of Mrs Hofland's books had been sold in England, and that the American sales were proportionately larger.[15]

Furthermore, we have to remember that Ramsay could not know of the enduring popularity of many of Mrs Hofland's works in England and overseas for half a century after her death. In England, for example, the firm of Arthur Hall, Virtue and Company, which took over from A.K. Newman, evidently found it profitable to produce what they called 'The Hofland Library' in the 1850s, publishing no fewer than 30 of Mrs Hofland's tales 'for the instruction and amusement of youth', handsomely bound in embossed scarlet cloth with gilt edges, and selling at either 2s. 6d. or 1s. 6d. each. Griffith and Farran included four of her books, *The Son of a Genius*, *The Daughter of a Genius*, *Ellen* and *Theodore, or the Crusaders*, as volumes IX, X, XI, and XII of 'The Favourite Library', which they published between 1871 and 1883. And Nelson & Sons republished at least eleven of her titles between 1866 and 1881. Similarly in America Mrs Hofland was still being published in the years after her death, and Chase & Nicoll of Boston produced a twelve-volume edition of her *Tales* in 1865.

The Young Crusoe is the most interesting example of Mrs Hofland's enduring popularity, as it is, of course, a witness to the major change in children's reading tastes in the middle of the nineteenth century when adventure stories and fantasies began to replace the moral tale. For though only three editions of this adventure story were published in her lifetime, the book was republished in England and America in at least ten different editions after her death. The last known was in Manchester in

1894, with a Preface by Alfonzo Gardiner.

The comments and reviews of critics throw considerable light on how Mrs Hofland's readers regarded her books.

It is important to remember, however, that, while the serious reviewing of adult novels was emerging at the beginning of the nineteenth century in such periodicals as the *Monthly Review* and the *Critical Review*, quarterlies like the *Edinburgh Review* or the great *Quarterly* itself did not review fiction regularly, and discussion of children's fiction lagged far behind.

Some reviews are little more than notices. Mrs Trimmer's *The Guardian of Education*, for example, which did take children's reading seriously and reviewed the works of Dr Aikin, Maria Edgeworth and Mme de Genlis, had ceased publication in 1806, before Mrs Hofland's children's tales had begun to appear. But *The Gentleman's Magazine*, *The Monthly* and *The Critical Review*, *The New Monthly* and *The Literary Gazette* all discussed Mrs Hofland's work from time to time, while *The Juvenile Review* (1817), a guide to parents and teachers in their choice of books, Lady Eastlake's long review-article on 'Children's Books' in the *Quarterly* in 1844, and later, Charlotte Yonge's fine essay on 'Children's Literature' published in *Macmillan's Magazine* in August 1869, all help to show what some of Mrs Hofland's readers thought of her work.[16]

The main quality the early reviewers praise Mrs Hofland for is her wholesome morality, the way in which her tales are framed so as to teach lessons which will help young readers to lead better lives.

Words like 'moral' and 'precept', often juxtaposed with 'excellent' and 'exemplary', occur and recur in the discussion of most children's books of this time, and it is quite clear that these are the qualities for which Mrs Hofland is praised.

But if the excellent morality of her books is the quality for which Mrs Hofland is most appreciated, at least up to the middle of the 1820s, the literary qualities of her books also gain a little recognition. *The Monthly Review* found *The Blind Farmer* 'both pleasing and pathetic',[17] and in a moment of unusual empathy *The British Critic* even imagined children reading the verses of *La Fête de la Rose* with pleasure. 'Young children, on their holidays, may be delightfully amused by them, ... A walk in the garden, with this book in the hand will be a very interesting entertainment.'[18]

This is not to say that Mrs Hofland's works escaped adverse comment completely, however, for though her books were usually well received, and her values never questioned, the reviewers were not afraid to point to weaknesses where they found them.

One has to be wary of generalising on the basis of such limited evidence, of course. Broadly speaking, Mrs Hofland's books received extremely favourable reviews, mainly because of their excellent moral teaching, and these reviews, on the whole, ignored literary weaknesses. Mrs Hofland's language was criticised occasionally for the negligent and grammatical errors which *The Monthly Review* found in *Says She to her Neighbour, What?*[19] but also for the defects of style which was 'so inflated' in *Ellen the Teacher*, the same magazine thought 'that children will scarcely understand it'.[20] The reviewer was mistaken here, as the book's large sales showed, but one suspects that he may have put his finger on one of the reasons for the declining popularity of many of the later books.

The most interesting review of Mrs Hofland's work, and one which in many ways marks a watershed in her career, is the review of *Integrity* which appeared in *The Literary Gazette* in April 1823. Something more than exemplary precepts are being used as critical touchstones by the reviewer, when he praises Mrs Hofland:

> At the end of one [volume], and that no very large book, Mrs. Hoffland (sic) contrives to dismiss her readers with the conviction of having passed some agreeable hours among people, most of

whom we should wish to imitate if we could, and at any rate are inclined to take the very first opportunity of making the attempt. Their characters are not likely to fade away from the mind very quickly, and their sentiments are too full of truth, and sometimes of delicacy and beauty not to make a lasting impression. We shall not attempt to narrate the story - we could not afford space enough to give it any interest. The character of Mr. Hastings, cold, arrogant, and puritannical in his prosperity, but softened, humbled, and even amiable in adversity, is well conceived and finely drawn; that of his wife, too, is of a superior description. Indeed the whole family of this name bears the stamp of nature and originality. The rest are perhaps ordinary beings, as found in Novels, but they are still men and women.[21]

What is happening, of course, is that taste and literary criteria are changing. Vitality, delicacy, beauty and realistic psychological development, among other qualities, are being praised by readers now, instead of the dogmatic certainties of the didactic moral fable, and the reviewer is reflecting this change in taste.

From now on the evidence suggests that Mrs Hofland's work received far less reviewing, and by the 1830s notices of her books seem to have declined to a mere trickle. This may be because such reviews as there were have not yet come to light, but the falling sales of Mrs Hofland's new books suggest that critics may have felt able to ignore them as other fiction came in to take their place, even though earlier books continued to be reprinted fairly frequently.

R.A. Colby has argued that all the major Victorian novels sprang to some extent from the didactic novels of the late eighteenth century, and suggests that they can often be best understood in relation to the popular if minor literature of the day.[22] The thesis is a useful one, and may suggest how Mrs Hofland's tales might have been read and used by some contemporaries and successors.

It is not difficult to see, for example, how Mrs Hofland's

stories of the patient and virtuous heroines, tested and tried by difficult circumstances, might have been taken up and developed in, for example, *Mansfield Park* and *Jane Eyre*.

Another of the recurring situations in Mrs Hofland's tales is one in which poor boys, often orphans or disadvantaged in some way, by their virtue and industry achieve prosperity and happiness. Ludovico's adventures in Leeds Market might have ended up in Fagin's Den, we feel, and the popularity in the first half of the nineteenth century of books like *The Son of a Genius* suggests that they may have played some small part in the making of such books as *Oliver Twist* and *David Copperfield*.

One of Mrs Hofland's greatest themes is the strength and the happiness of family life. Her most powerful and recurring motif is the demonstration of family love and co-operation in the face of some crisis or disaster, the loss of a parent, for instance, and one can only speculate on the possibility of the influence of her work on, for example, Charlotte Yonge's *The Daisy Chain* (1856), Louisa Alcott's *Little Women* (1868) and *The Railway Children* (1906) by Mrs Nesbit.

But the evidence is elusive, as it is for more specific influences. What we do know is that Mrs Hofland's works were read and enjoyed for their own sakes for well over half a century, in England, Europe and America, and that she helped to create the great tradition of children's literature which went on to include Lewis Carroll and R.L. Stevenson, Frances Hodgson Burnett and Mrs Nesbit, a tradition in which, despite her faults, she deserves a small but honourable place.

Notes

1. R.D. Altick, *The English Common Reader : A social history of the mass reading public 1800-1900*, Chicago, 1967, p.264.
2. Dorothy Blakey, *The Minerva Press 1790-1820*, Oxford, 1939, pp.73-5.
3. Mrs Hofland to R.L. Edgeworth, 29 June 1815, Colvin Collection.
4. Thomas Ramsay, *The Life and Literary Remains of Barbara Hofland*, London, 1849, p.viii, says, for example, that *The Clergyman's Widow* sold 17,000 copies in various editions.
5. Mrs Hofland to R.L. Edgeworth, 29 June 1815, Colvin Collection.
6. M. Moon, *John Harris's Books for Youth 1801-1843*, (1983), with supplement, Winchester, 1987.
7. The Longman Archives are lodged with Reading University, through whose courtesy these figures are quoted. I use the generic term Longmans for the frequently changing team of this publishing house, but for further details see E. Cox and J.E. Chandler, *The House of Longman 1724-1924*, London, 1925.
8. In 1831, for example, the earnings for *Moderation* came to £1 6s. 2d. and for *Self-Denial* in 1832 to £0 4s. 4d.
9. For Maria Edgeworth's literary income, see M. Butler, *Maria Edgeworth: A literary biography*, Oxford, 1972, p.492; and for Charlotte Smith, see A.D. McKillop, 'Charlotte Smith's Letters', *Huntingdon Library Quarterly*, vol. 15, 1952, pp.237-55.
10. See Alison Adburgham, *Women in Print; Writing Women and Women's Magazines from the Restoration to the Accession of Victoria*, London, 1972, p.257; Andrew Boyle, *An Index to the Annuals*, Worcester, 1967, I, pp.129-30.
11. *The Letters of M.R. Mitford*, second series, ed. H. Chorley, 2 vols, London, 1872, I, pp.267-68.
12. *The Life and Letters of Maria Edgeworth*, ed. Augustus J.C. Hare, 2 vols, London, 1894, I, p.305.
13. *The Son of a Genius*, 'New Edition' 1836, p.iv.
14. See *Catalogue Général des livres imprimés de la Bibliothèque Nationale*, Paris, 1920, vol 72, and *The National Union Catalogue Pre-1956 Imprints*, London, 1973, vol 250.
15. Thomas Ramsay, *op.cit.*, p.viii.
16. A fuller checklist of contemporary reviews of Mrs Hofland's work is included in Chapter IV.
17. *Monthly Review*, 80, July 1816, p.324.
18. *The British Critic*, XXXIV, July 1809, pp.69-70.

19 *Monthly Review*, 69, September 1812, pp.96-7.
20 *Monthly Review*, 80, May 1816, p.96.
21 *The Literary Gazette; and Journal of Belles Lettres*, 327, 26 April 1823, pp.259-60.
22 R.A. Colby, *Fiction with a Purpose*, Indiana, 1967.

4 Mrs Hofland's Books

Any attempt to draw up even a provisional checklist of Mrs Hofland's works is fraught with considerable difficulties. Books discussed by Mrs Hofland in letters, or mentioned by friends, have sometimes disappeared without trace, while others not mentioned by her or her biographer Thomas Ramsay clearly have her name on the title-page. Some books published anonymously are demonstrably by Mrs Hofland, while others have been wrongly attributed to her. In two cases no known copies of a work survive, in another no first edition has yet been located, and in others single copies only have been found. The dating of several undated works also presents problems. In the absence of journals or substantial correspondence, with publishing records scanty, and with so many gaps in Ramsay's biography, it is not surprising that such authorities as Block, the *Cambridge Bibliography*, and Halkett and Laing are sometimes inaccurate, omitting some works by Mrs Hofland, attributing other work to her on doubtful evidence, and occasionally misdating books.

What this checklist aims to do, therefore, is to provide as

accurate and complete a record as possible at the present time of Mrs Hofland's English publications in book form, including short but independent pamphlets but omitting contributions to periodicals, and books first published overseas. It gives the date and other details of first publication, together with a brief publishing history of subsequent editions, when known, to show Mrs Hofland's enduring and international reputation almost to the end of the nineteenth century. Discussion of some controversial attributions, information about Mrs Hofland's work for the *Annuals* and Pocket Books, and details of many contemporary reviews of Mrs Hofland's works, are given at the end of the checklist.

Notes on the arrangement of entries

Sequence The bibliography is arranged chronologically in order of publication.

The title-page and, where appropriate, engraved title-page, of First Editions are quoted in full, except for quotations, but the typography has not been imitated.

The dating of books Where the date of publication is not printed on the title-page or elsewhere in a book, the arguments for deciding a particular date are given in the notes below the listing of the title-page, and are based upon internal evidence - dates of illustrations or advertisements, and external evidence - letters and publishers' catalogues.

Measurements are of title-leaves of First Editions, but minor variations are frequent in rebound copies, and are only noted where particularly significant.

Pagination shows a full account of all pages, and unless stated otherwise, it should be assumed that frontispiece and illustrations are additional.

Printers The name and address are normally taken from the verso of the title-leaf or the end of the book, unless the printer's name is given on the title-page.

Bindings Original bindings are described, where possible, but only the more interesting examples of rebindings are noted.

Locations Square brackets enclose the names and symbols denoting the locations of some recorded copies, but these must not be regarded as a census of all existing copies of a book.

Notes Evidence for dating a book, if necessary, together with supplementary information about make-up and contents, and a summary of each book's publishing history as far as is known.

Abbreviations and locations of first and other important editions

ABER	Aberdeen University Library
AC	Author's collection
BELL	Mr and Mrs D. Bell, private collection, Newent, Glos.
BIB	*Catalogue Général des livres imprimés de la Bibliothèque Nationale*, vol 72, Paris, 1920.
BLOCK	Andrew Block, *The English Novel 1740-1850*, rev. edn, Dawsons, London, 1963.
BL	British Library
BOD	Bodleian Library, Oxford
CBEL	*The New Cambridge Bibliography of English Literature*, ed. George Watson, 5 vols, Cambridge University Press, 1974-77.
DARTON	F.J. Harvey Darton, *Children's Books in England: five centuries of social life*, third edn, revised by Brian Alderson, Cambridge University Press, 1982.
EC	*The English Catalogue of Printed Books 1801-1836* (preliminary volume) *The English Catalogue of Printed Books 1835-1863*, vol I *The English Catalogue of Printed Books 1863-1871*, vol II *The English Catalogue of Printed Books 1872-1880*, vol III *The English Catalogue of Printed Books 1881-1889*, vol IV All volumes published by Kraus Reprints, New York, 1963.

GUMUCHIAN	Gumuchian & Cie, *Les Livres de L'Enfance du XVe au XIXe Siècle*, 2 vols, Paris (1930)
H & L	Samuel Halkett and John Laing, *Dictionary of Anonymous and Pseudonymous English Literature*, New and Enlarged Edition, eds J. Kennedy and W.A. Smith, 9 vols, Oliver & Boyd, London, 1926-62.
HARROGATE	North Yorkshire County Library, Harrogate
LILLY	Lilly Library, Indiana University, Bloomington, USA
LONGMAN	Longman Archive, Reading University
MOON	Marjorie Moon, *John Harris's Books for Youth 1801-1843*, (1983), with supplement, St Paul's Bibliographies, Winchester, 1987
NATIONAL ART	National Art Library, Victoria and Albert Museum, London
NUC	*National Union Catalogue Pre-1956*, vol. 250, Mansell, London
OSB	*The Catalogue of the Osborne Collection of Children's Books*, 2 vols, Toronto Public Library, Toronto, 1958-75
QUAYLE	Eric Quayle, private collection, Zennor, Cornwall
RAMSAY	Thomas Ramsay, *The Life and Literary Remains of Barbara Hoffland*, W.J. Cleaver, London, 1849
READING LIB	Reading Public Library
READING UNIV	Reading University Library

RENIER   Renier Collection of Children's Books,
                    Bethnal Green Museum of Childhood,
                    London
RUSSELL   June Russell, *Bibliography of Barbara
                    Hofland*, Sheffield City Library, 1950
SHEFFIELD   Sheffield City Library
SOANE   Sir John Soane Museum Library,
                    London

Abbreviations used in descriptions of the books

Advert	advertisement
a.e.g.	all edges gilt
cm.	centimetres
del.	drew
Decr.	December
f.e.p.	front end paper
n.d.	no date, undated
P. Pp.	page, pages
Pubd.	published
Sc., sculp.	engraved
verso front cover	inside front cover
vol.	volume

Chronological listing

The books are listed in order of publication, but where several books were published in the same year, and exact dates are not known, they are listed in alphabetical order.

1805

1   POEMS, by Barbara Hoole | 3 lines by Spenser | engraving of ruined abbey | Sheffield: Printed by J. Montgomery, at the *Iris* Office, And sold by Vernor and Hood, Booksellers in the Poultry, London.

16 × 10.5 cm. Pp. xlvii (including advertisement dated May 5th, 1805, p iv) + 256. AC and BL, calf with raised bands, gilt lettering and decoration with *Hoole's Poems* on spine on black label. SHEFFIELD rebound in library binding c.1926.

[AC, BL, SHEFFIELD]

The Advertisement, pp. (iii)-iv, is dated May 5, 1805; *The Iris* said copies were ready on May 30th. The names of the subscribers, listed on pp. (v)-xlvii, show that 1,620 purchased 2,040 copies between them at 6s. each.

1809

2   LA FETE DE LA ROSE; or, the Dramatic Flowers. A holiday present for young people. By Mrs B. Hoole. Sheffield: Printed by J. Montgomery, Iris Office; for Longman, Hurst, Rees and Orme, London. 1809.

13 × 12.1 cm. Pp. 22. Rose-coloured paper wrappers entitled LA FETE DE LA ROSE | vignette of flowers in urn | OR, THE DRAMATIC FLOWERS | vignette of flowers in vase.

[SHEFFIELD]

NUC records a second edition, also by Longman, in 1809, and *OSB* notes a third edition in 1810. (DARTON [p. 210] says second and third editions appeared in 1810). The Longman Archive shows that 70 (further?) copies were received for sale in March 1813, and that only 24 remained in June 1814.

3   THE HISTORY OF AN OFFICER'S WIDOW, AND HER YOUNG FAMILY | Quotation from Congreve | London: Printed for J. Harris (Successor to E. Newberry) Corner of St. Paul's Church Yard. 1809.

16.8 × 10 cm. Printed by W. Wilson, St. John's Square. Pp. vii + 182. BL rebound in marbled boards, SHEFFIELD in modern library binding c. 1926.

[BL, SHEFFIELD]

MOON cites a second edition of 1812, third of 1814, and 'New Editions' by John Harris in 1818, 1820, 1823, c.1830 and 1834. Additionally, *NUC* records two Boston editions (n.d. and 1865), two in New York (1815 and 1846), and one in Philadelphia (1815).

1810

4   LITTLE DRAMAS FOR YOUNG PEOPLE, on subjects taken from English History: Intended to Promote Among the Rising Generation an Early Love of Virtue and their Country. By Mrs. B. Hoole, Author of "La Fete de la Rose," & c. | 4 lines from Cowper | London: Printed for Longman, Hurst, Rees and Orme. Sold by A. and E. Gales, Sheffield; and Hargrove, Knaresborough and Harrogate. 1810

18 × 10 cm. Printed by T. Davison, Whitefriars, London. Pp. vii (including Preface dated 'Boarding school, Harrogate, October 20th, 1809' p vii) + Pp 128. READING UNIV boards repaired, BL and SHEFFIELD in modern rebinding.

[BL, READING UNIV, SHEFFIELD]

The *Preface* is dated October 20th, 1809, and the Longman Archive shows that 750 copies were actually published on December 14th, 1809. The book sold steadily at 1s. 9d. per copy, and only 20 were left by June 1814; these were remaindered at 6½d. each.

5   TALES, IN VERSE, for the use of children, of both sexes, designed for a Midsummer present. Knaresborough: Printed by Hargrove and Sons; for Longman, Hurst, Rees, and Orme, Paternoster-Row; Sold by Tabart and Co., London; Hargrove and Sons, Knaresborough and Harrogate; Wilson and Son,

58 Barbara Hofland

and Todd and Sons, York; and all other booksellers. 1810.

13.5 × 11.3 cm. Pp. 24, including a Dedication to the infant daughters of James Wolf Murray signed by Barbara Hofland, and dated 'Boarding-School, Harrogate, June 13.' The LILLY copy in green morocco, stamped in gold with marbled endpapers, has the original pink wrappers bound in. The front wrapper within decorated border reads TALES, in Verse, | vignette of bird on branch of tree | For the Use of Children of both Sexes. | vignette of horse drinking. The rear wrapper within decorated border reads | vignette of tree | A Midsummer Present, | decorative device | For Children, | vignette of ruined building | Hargroves, Knaresborough.

[LILLY]

1812

6   THE DAUGHTER-IN-LAW
No copy of the first edition is known, and *CBEL* dates the tale as 1829. But the book is referred to on the title-page of the first edition of *The Son of a Genius* (1812) as by the same author. *The Gentleman's Magazine* (vol. 23, January 1845) even says it was the first book written after the Hoflands moved to London, and was much admired by Queen Charlotte. It is also included among advertisements of the publisher Newman's other publications in *Patience and Perseverance* (see 12 below) in 1813. For these reasons an edition of 1812 seems likely. *NUC* cites a 'New Edition' in Harvard University Library (Cambridge, Mass., USA) published by A.K. Newman in 1825; the earliest edition examined was the BL copy as follows:

THE DAUGHTER-IN-LAW, HER FATHER, AND FAMILY. By Mrs. Hofland, author of the Clergyman's Widow; Merchant's Widow; Blind Farmer; Barbadoes Girl; Affectionate Brothers; Sisters; Young Northern Traveller; Young Crusoe; Good Grandmother; Panorama of Europe; &c. &c. | Quotation from Fordyce's Sermons | New Edition. London: Printed for A.K. Newman and Co. 1829.

13.8 × 8.2 cm. Printed by J. Darling, Leadenhall Street, London. Engraved frontispiece E. Burney Del, Engraved in Steel by S. Springsguth. Engraved abbreviated t.p. THE DAUGHTER-IN-LAW, her Father & Family. By Mrs. Hofland, author of Affectionate Brothers, Merchant's Widow, Blind Farmer, Panorama of Europe, Barbadoes Girl, the Sisters, Clergyman's Widow, Young

Northern Traveller, Good Grandmother, Young Crusoe, &c. &c. London. Printed for A.K. Newman & Co. Pp. 196. BL copy rebound in library binding.

Later copies include a 'New Edition' in SHEFFIELD, undated but referring to *The Stolen Boy* of 1830, and so probably of that date. The book was apparently last published in 'The Hofland Library' by Arthur Hall, Virtue & Co., dated by the advertisements January 1st, 1853 (AC).

[AC, BL, SHEFFIELD]

7   THE HISTORY OF A CLERGYMAN'S WIDOW AND HER YOUNG FAMILY. By the author of an Officer's Widow and her Young Family | 3 lines by Akenside | London: Printed at the Minerva-Press, for A.K. Newman and Co. Leadenhall Street. 1812.

18.5 x 10.1 cm. Printed by Lane, Darling and Co., Leadenhall-Street. Engraved frontispiece headed 'An Interesting Scene from' (sic). Pp. (i) + 240. BL copy rebound.

[BL]

This was one of Mrs. Hofland's most popular books; a second edition was published in 1814, and the story, sometimes retitled *The Clergyman's Widow*, had reached its seventh edition for Newman by 1825 (BELL). *NUC* cites editions in Boston (182?, 1855? and 1865), New York (1830) and Philadelphia (1875): and *CBEL* records a French translation of 1831.*

The book was reprinted in 'The Hofland Library' by Hall, Virtue and Co. in the 1850s, and later English editions include Nelson 1866 (BOD), and another in 1867 (*EC*, vol II) presumably the same as the one listed by *CBEL*.

8   SAYS SHE TO HER NEIGHBOUR, *What?* In Four Volumes. By an Old-Fashioned Englishman. | 6 lines of poetry (from Barbara Hofland's 'Lines

---

* Very little is known of translations of Mrs Hofland's works. Chapter two of *Alfred Campbell* (1825) describes a visit to the Protestant Church in Paris to hear a sermon by M. Monod, and a footnote adds, 'The daughter of this gentleman, now Madame Bubethas, translated several works of the present author into French.' (p.11). The 'revised edition' of 1841 says she is 'now Madame Babet' (p.11).

Addressed to Mr. Erskine' *Poems*, pp. 192-3) | Vol 1. London: Printed at the Minerva-Press, for A.K. Newman and Co. Leadenhall-Street. 1812.

17 × 10.3 cm. Printed by Lane, Darling & Co., Leadenhall-Street, London. Pp. 285 + iii advertising 'New Publications printed for A.K. Newman & Co. at the Minerva-Press, Leadenhall-Street, London' - Vol. I; Pp 291 + i advertising 'New Publications printed for A.K. Newman & Co. at the Minerva-Press, Leadenhall-Street, London' - Vol. II; Pp 336 - Vol. III; Pp 336 - Vol. IV. BL, SHEFFIELD have four volumes rebound separately in library binding, the latter c.1926. QUAYLE has four volumes rebound as two.

[BL, QUAYLE, SHEFFIELD]

NUC records a New York edition of 1815.

9   A SEASON AT HARROGATE; in a series of poetical epistles, from Benjamin Blunderhead, Esquire, to his mother, in Derbyshire: With useful and copious notes, descriptive of the objects most worthy of attention in the vicinity of Harrogate | 1 line by Pope | Knaresborough: Printed by G. Wilson and sold by R. Wilson, Knaresborough, and Harrogate: Longman, Hurst, Rees, Orme, and Brown, Paternoster Row, London; Robinson, Heaton, L. & I. Nicholls, and Baines, Leeds; Wolstenholme, and Todd, York; Hunsley and Thomas, Doncaster; Langdale, Rippon; Edwards, Halifax; Miss Gales, Sheffield; and Wright, Liverpool. 1812.

21.2 × 12.7 cm. Pp. vii (including advertisement by B. Hofland, dated December 1, 1811) + Pp. 103. READING UNIV has boards with 'HARROGATE' on spine; BL, BOD and SHEFFIELD rebound.

[BL, BOD, HARROGATE, READING UNIV, SHEFFIELD]

The Longman Archive records receipt of 100 copies in May 1812, of which 85 had been sold by March 1816, with Wilson of Harrogate receiving 10 per cent of the sales. New editions were published in Harrogate in 1838 and 1904 [HARROGATE].

10   THE SON OF A GENIUS; a Tale for the use of Youth. By the Author of the History of an Officer's Widow and Family, Clergyman's Widow and

Family, Daughter in Law. &c. &c. | Quotation from Proverbs | London: Printed for J. Harris, Corner of St. Paul's Church-Yard; and B. and R. Crosby, Stationers' Court, 1812.

16.3 × 10.2 cm. Printed by R. Hemstead, Great New Street, Gough Square. Engraved Frontispiece dated October 20 - 1812. Pp. vii + Pp. 251 + 4 pp. advertising Harris's recent publications and New Year Gifts. BOD rebound. (P [iii] is addressed to F.P.N. - 'The Author's Son' and p. vii is signed B.N.,the printer presumably misreading H for N.)

[BOD]

This was the most popular of all Mrs Hofland's books. MOON cites other editions published by Harris appearing in 1816, 1817, 1818, 1819, 1821, 1822, 1823, 1825, 1827, 1830, 1832 and 1841 ('14th edn.').

The missing edition of 1826 is recorded by BELL as 'Carefully Revised and Enlarged by the Author', and with no date on the title-page but a new Dedication to the Author's son dated October 10, 1826.

NUC confirms that the book was enormously popular in America and cites editions in New York (1814, 1818, 1832, 1839, 1860), in Boston (1826, 1865), and in Ohio (1852, 1853). *BIB* notes no fewer than five French editions, the earliest as follows:

Ludovico, ou le fils d'un homme de genie, traduit de l'anglais par Mme la Baronne de Montolieu, Paris, A. Bertrand, 1817.

This was reprinted in 1821 and 1833, and there were also English versions published in Paris in 1829 and 1840, the latter as Vol. 44 of Baudry's 'European' and 'Juvenile Library'.

Later English editions include the 'Fifteenth edn.' of Grant and Griffiths, 1850, Griffith and Farran's 'Favourite Library' No. LX of 1879, and their 'new edition' of 1886 (*EC*, vol. iv).

1813

11 IWANOWNA; or, the Maid of Moscow. A novel. In Two Volumes. By the Author of the Clergyman's Widow, Officer's Widow, Son of a Genius, Sisters, &c. | Quotation of 8 lines by Montgomery | Vol. I. London: Printed for G. and S. Robinson, Paternoster Row. 1813.

16 × 9.5 cm. Vol. I printed by T. Davison, Lombard Street, Fleet Street, London; Vol. II printed by J. Moyes, Greville Street, Hatton Gardens, London.

Pp. 265 - Vol. I; Pp. 279 - Vol. II. BL and SHEFFIELD both rebound.

[BL, SHEFFIELD]

NUC records editions in Philadelphia (1815) and New York (1816).

12   THE PANORAMA OF EUROPE; or, a new game of Geography. By the author of the Officer's Widow; Clergyman's Widow; Daughter-in-Law; Little Dramas; Son of a Genius; Sisters; Northern Tourist, &c. &c. | 6 lines by Cowper | London: Printed at the Minerva-Press, for A.K. Newman and Co. Leadenhall-Street. 1813.

18.4 x 10.7 cm. Printed by J. Darling, Leadenhall-Street, London. Engraved frontispiece. Hetz (?) del., Walker sculp. Pp. (iv) (with 'To Sophia, the daughter of the Rev. Theophilus Lant, Lewisham Hill' dated March 3, 1813, p. iii) + 240. BL and SHEFFIELD both rebound, the latter in library binding c.1926.

[BL, SHEFFIELD]

NUC cites a second edition in 1819, a fourth in 1824, and a sixth in 1828. BOD has an eighth edition dated March 18, 1836, and the last known edition seems to be that cited for 1840 by *CBEL*.

13   PATIENCE AND PERSEVERANCE; or, the Modern Griselda. A domestic tale. In four volumes. By the author of *Says she to her neighbour, What?* & c. 5 lines by Thomson | Vol. I. London: Printed at the Minerva-Press, for A.K. Newman and Co. Leadenhall-Street. 1813.

18.3 x 10.5 cm. Printed by J. Darling, Leadenhall-Street, London. Pp iii + 283 (+ 1 advertising 'New Publications Printed for A.K. Newman & Co. at the Minerva Press, Leadenhall-Street, London.') - Vol I; Pp 282 + 2 pp advertising 'New Publications Printed for A.K. Newman & Co. at the Minerva Press, Leadenhall-Street, London' - Vol II; Pp 262 + 2 pp advertising 'New Publications Printed for A.K. Newman & Co. at the Minerva Press, Leadenhall-Street, London' - Vol. III; Pp 223 (+ 1 p advertising 'New Publications Printed for A.K. Newman & Co. at the Minerva-Press, Leadenhall-Street, London.') - Vol. IV. SHEFFIELD has four volumes rebound separately in modern library binding c.1926, BL four volumes rebound as one.

[BL, SHEFFIELD]

NUC records one American edition only: Philadelphia in 1816.

14   THE SISTERS; a dramatic tale, by the author of the Officer's Widow and Family; Clergyman's Widow and Family; Little Dramas, &c. &c. Quotation from Zimmerman | Ipswich: Printed by J. Raw, and sold by Longman, Hurst, Rees, Orme and Brown, London. 1813.

16.5 x 9.5 cm. Pp 249 + pp 12 (dated April 1813) advertising 'Established School Books, printed for Longman, Hurst, Rees, Orme, and Brown, Paternoster Row.' BL in calf with gold bands on spine, SHEFFIELD rebound in modern library binding c.1926.

[BL, SHEFFIELD]

The history of this book is complicated, and suggests that the *CBEL* entry needs revising. It was evidently first printed by J. Raw of Ipswich but sold by Longman in London in 1813, though no record of this survives in the Longman Archive. Within a year the book was republished by the Minerva Press, with no mention of earlier publication.

The Sisters. A Domestic Tale by Mrs. Hofland, Author of The Clergyman's Widow .... &c. &c. London: Printed at the Minerva-Press for A.K. Newman and Co., 1814. Pp 249.

[READING UNIV]

Without recording either of these editions *CBEL* cites 1828 as the date of the first printing, with later editions of (1830?) and 1866 (attributed by *EC*, vol. II, to Nelson), and a French translation of 1832. GUMUCHIAN cites an edition of c.1840 by Arthur Hall. *NUC* records editions in Hartford (1815), Boston (1865) and Philadelphia (187?). *The Sisters* was advertised in 'The Hofland Library' in the 1850s and the last English edition seems to have been published by Nelson in 1866 (AC).

15   THE YOUNG NORTHERN TRAVELLER. Being a series of letters from Frederick to Charles, during a tour through the north of Europe. By the author

of The Officer's Widow and Family; the Clergyman's Widow and Family; the Daughter-in-Law, &c. London: Printed at the Minerva-Press, for A.K. Newman and Co. Leadenhall-Street. 1813.

17.7 × 10.5 cm. Printed by Lane, Darling, & Co. Leadenhall-Street, London. Engraved frontispiece Metz del., Heath sculp, Pp 176. SHEFFIELD rebound in modern library binding c.1926.

[SHEFFIELD]

Later Mrs. Hofland produced a revised edition: THE YOUNG NORTHERN TRAVELLER; or, the Invalid Restored. Containing a tour through Northern Europe, with historical and biographical anecdotes. By Mrs. Hofland, author of the Clergyman's Widow; Merchant's Widow; Blind Farmer; Barbadoes Girl; Affectionate Brothers; Sisters; Good Grandmother; Panorama of Europe; Young Crusoe; Daughter-in-Law; &c. &c. New Edition, With additions and alterations. London: Printed for A.K. Newman and Co. (n.d.)

13.9 × 8.5 cm. Printed by J. Darling, Leadenhall Street. Engraved frontispiece, E. Burney del., S. Springsguth Sculp. Engraved abbreviated t.p. THE YOUNG NORTHERN TRAVELLER, or, the Invalid Restored. By Mrs. Hofland. Author of Affectionate Brothers Good Grandmother Barbadoes Girl Merchants Widow Blind Farmer Panorama of Europe Clergymans Widow Sisters Daughter in Law Young Crusoe &c. &c. London. Printed for A.K. Newman & Co. Pp ii (Contents) + ii ('To the Reader,' explaining how the work has been rewritten from its previous epistolary form) + 175 (+ 1 advertising 'New Publications for the Instruction and Amusement of Youth, sold by A.K. Newman and Co. London.') with some works [e.g. *Fashionable Letter Writer*] dated 1829. SHEFFIELD has marbled boards, red roan spine, with gilt lettering *'Hofland's Traveller'*.

[SHEFFIELD]

Advertisements for other publications by Newman within this volume date it as not earlier than 1829, and advertisements in a BL copy date that as post-1835. *BIB* notes a French edition of 1834, and *CBEL* records a French translation of 1825. The book also appeared in 'The Hofland Library' in the 1850s.

1814

16 ELLEN, THE TEACHER. A tale for Youth. By Mrs. Hofland, Author of the Officer's Widow; Son of a Genius; and other works for young people. | 1 line by Shakespeare | Vol. I London: Printed for J. Harris, the Corner of St. Paul's Church-Yard. 1814.

13 x 8 cm. Printed by H. Bryer, Bridge-street, Blackfriars, London. Engraved frontispiece to each vol. pubd. Sept. 20, 1814. by J. Harris, corner of St. Paul's Churchyard, frontispiece illustrating p 134, Vol. I and p 22, Vol. II. Pp 180 - Vol. I; Pp. 171 - Vol. II. SHEFFIELD has both volumes rebound in modern library binding c.1926.

[SHEFFIELD]

This was one of Mrs Hofland's most popular books, and MOON cites editions published by Harris in 1819 ('2nd edn.'), 1822 ('3rd edn.'), 1824, 1825, 1829, 1833, 1836 and 1841. *NUC* cites copies in New York in 1815, 1819, and 187? and in Boston in 1863 and 1865, and *BIB* records three French editions in Paris: 1817, 1827 and 1835.

Griffith and Farran published the book as Volume XI in 'The Favourite Library', with no date, but BOD's copy has a list at the back dated September 1879, and *EC* (Vol. iv) records a 'new edition' of 1886.

17 THE MERCHANT'S WIDOW AND HER FAMILY. By the author of The Officer's Widow and her Family; Clergyman's Widow and Family; Daughter-in-Law, &c. | 4 lines by Dr. Johnson | London: Printed at the Minerva-Press, for A.K. Newman and Co. Leadenhall-Street. 1814.

19 x 11 cm. Printed by J. Darling. Engraved frontispiece. Pp iii + 236. SOANE in blue cloth-covered boards with label on spine reading *The Merchant's Widow and her Family*, Price 4s. 1814. SOANE is Sir John Soane's own copy with his signature and the inscription 'Sat: 24 Sept: 1814 I first heard of this novel and it was purchased on Monday the 26th.' (The novel contains Mrs Hofland's warm praise of the architect pp 76-80). BL in plain boards lacking spine.

[BL, SOANE]

Another of Mrs Hofland's most popular tales, sometimes retitled *The History of a Merchant's Widow and her Young Family*, the second edition was published by the Minerva Press in 1818 (RENIER). *CBEL* cites later English editions in 1823 and 1826 (the sixth according to *NUC*) and 1857, and *BIB* a French edition of 1831. *NUC* records publication in Boston in 182? and New York in 1830 and 1839. The book was advertised in 'The Hofland Library' in the 1850s (perhaps the *CBEL* edition of 1857?), and the last English editions seem to be those by Nelson in 1865 (*EC*, vol. ii) and in 1868, according to *NUC*.

18   A VISIT TO LONDON, or Emily and her Friends. Four Vols. London: the Minerva Press, 1814.

No copy of this book is known, but RAMSAY says that Queen Charlotte was so impressed by *The Daughter-in-Law* that she signified her permission that a future work might be dedicated to her, and that this was the book.

Mrs. Hofland's letter dated 20 January 1812, discusses the date of the book's publication and the wording of the Dedication to the Queen. (BOD, Ms. Montagu d 7). Robert Watt in his *Bibliotheca Britannica*, 4 vols, Edinburgh, 1824, records the book as published in four volumes in 1814, at 24/- (vol. I, p. 504x), and Dorothy Blakey (*The Minerva Press*, Oxford 1939) also attributes the work to Mrs Hofland.

1815

19   A FATHER as he should be. A Novel. In Four Volumes. By Mrs. Hofland, Author of Says She to her Neighbour, Clergyman's Widow, Visit to London, Patience and Perseverance, &c. &c. | 5 lines from *The Rambler* | Vol. I. London: Printed at the Minerva-Press, for A.K. Newman and Co. Leadenhall-Street. 1815.

16.7 × 10cm. Printed by J. Darling, Leadenhall-Street, London. Pp. (i) (dedication 'To Her Royal Highness the Princess Elizabeth') + 262 - Vol. I; Pp. 276 - Vol. II; Pp. 274 + pp. 2 advertising 'New Publications Printed for A.K. Newman & Co. at the Minerva Press, Leadenhall-Street, London.' - Vol. III; Pp. 291 (+ 1 p. advertising 'New Publications Printed at the Minerva Press, Leadenhall Street, London') - Vol. IV. SHEFFIELD has all four volumes rebound in modern library binding c. 1926, BL has four volumes rebound as one volume.

[BL, SHEFFIELD]

In addition to a second edition published by Newman in 1824, *NUC* also records an American edition published in Philadelphia in 1816.

1816

20   THE AFFECTIONATE BROTHERS. A Tale. In Two Volumes. By Mrs. Hofland, Author of the Clergyman's Widow, the Panorama of Europe, &c. &c. | 7 lines from Beattie | Vol. I. London : Printed at the Minerva Press for A.K. Newman and Co. Leadenhall-Street. 1816.

13.6 x 8.5 cm. Printed by J. Darling, 31, Leadenhall-Street, London. Engraved frontispiece. Pp. 140 - Vol. I; Pp. 134 - Vol. II + pp 2 advertising 'The Following New Publications,' which includes *Visit to London, or Emily and her Friends*, by Mrs. Hofland, 4 vols. £1-4-0. BL in marbled boards, red roan spine, with gilt bands and gilt lettering on spine of title *Affectionate Brothers* SHEFFIELD rebound in modern library binding c.1926.

[BL, SHEFFIELD]

CBEL cites later editions in 1829, 1835 (?) and 1863, while *NUC* records American editions in New York (1816, 1819, 1851), Albany (1818?), and Boston (1831, 1865). The book was advertised in 'The Hofland Library' in the 1850s, and later English editions include one published by Nelson in 1869 (BELL), and one by Goubaud in 1878 (*EC*, vol. iii).

21   THE BLIND FARMER AND HIS CHILDREN. By Mrs. Hofland. Author of the Son of a Genius, - Officer's Widow, - Clergyman's Widow, - Sisters, - Ellen the Teacher, - Affectionate Brothers, &c. &c | 3 lines from Thomson | London: Printed for J. Harris, Corner of St. Paul's Church-Yard. 1816.

16.3 x 9.5 cm. Printed by H. Bryer, Bridge-Street, Blackfriars, London. Engraved frontispiece published Dec. 1 - 1815 by J. Harris corner of St. Pauls. Pp iv + 183 + pp 8 advertisements 'Of J. Harris Corner of St. Paul's'. BL calf with gilt bands on spine, SHEFFIELD rebound in modern library binding.

[BL, SHEFFIELD]

MOON cites three other editions by Harris; the second 1819; third 1823; fourth 1825; the *CBEL* notes a sixth of 1830 (?), and *NUC* a seventh by Newman in 1831 (?) as well as American editions in Albany in 1817, New York in 1831, 1850 (?) and 1851, and a Boston edition of 1865. Reprinted in 'The Hofland Library' in the 1850s, the book was last published by Nelson in 1872 according to an inscription (BELL).

22   MATILDA; or the Barbadoes Girl. A Tale for Young People. By the Author of the Clergyman's Widow and Family, Merchant's Widow and Family, Affectionate Brothers, Panorama of Europe, the Sisters, &c. | quotations from Bacon and Addison | London: Printed at the Minerva Press for A.K. Newman and Co. Leadenhall-street. 1816.

17.5 × 9.8 cm. Printed by J. Darling, Leadenhall-Street, London. Engraved frontispiece. Pp. 250. BL rebound with *Mary and Fanny* by Juvenis, 1816, SHEFFIELD rebound in library binding c.1926.

[BL, SHEFFIELD]

This book, sometimes reprinted as *The Barbadoes Girl*, was republished in 1819 according to *CBEL*, and in 1824 (READING UNIV), and had reached a fifth edition by 1825 (?) according to *NUC*. Advertisements in the *National Art Library* copy date it 1837, and the book also appears in 'The Hofland Library' in the 1850s. *NUC* records publication in Philadelphia in 1817, New York in 1831, and Boston in 1865, and *BIB* an edition in Paris in 1865. The last English edition appears to be that cited by *CBEL* in 1866.

1817

23   THE FUNERAL. A monody to the memory of the Princess Charlotte. By Mrs. Hofland | vignette of weeping willow leaning over a watery shore | Sheffield: Printed by Bentham and Ray (n.d.)

19.1 × 12.3 cm. Printed by Bentham and Ray, High-Street, Sheffield. Pp. 10. Paper wrappers with t.p. as cover.

[SHEFFIELD]

Princess Charlotte died on 5 November 1817, and was buried at Windsor on 19

November so it seems reasonable to date this item 1817. It is not recorded in *CBEL*, etc., and the Sheffield copy appears to be the unique survivor, though it was also published in *The Northern Star* in January 1818.

24 THE GOOD GRANDMOTHER, AND HER OFFSPRING; a Tale by Mrs. Hofland, Author of "The Son of a Genius", &c. &c. | Quotation from Proverbs | London: Printed for R. Hunter, (Successor to Mr. Johnson) St. Paul's Church-Yard. 1817.

17.6 x 9.7 cm. Printed by G. Woodfall, Angel Court, Skinner Street, London. Pp iv + 164. BL rebound with *The Story of Clarissa*, 1817; *The Canary Bird* by Alicia Catherine Mant, 1812; and *The Exile*, (anon.) 1820. SHEFFIELD rebound in modern library binding c.1926.

[BL, SHEFFIELD]

A second edition was published by Newman in 1828 (READING UNIV), reprinted in the 1830s (AC), and *CBEL* also cites an edition of 1850. *NUC* records editions in New York (1817, 1852), Boston (1821, 1840 and 1865) and Newburyport (1833). The book was advertised in 'The Hofland Library' in the 1850s, and the last English edition of the 1860s (?) published by Nelson is in the Renier Collection.

1819

25 A DESCRIPTIVE ACCOUNT OF THE MANSION AND GARDENS OF WHITE-KNIGHTS, a Seat of His Grace the Duke of Marlborough. By Mrs. Hofland. Illustrated with Twenty-Three Engravings, from pictures taken on the Spot by T.C. Hofland | 2 lines from Thomson | London: Printed for His Grace the Duke of Marlborough by W. Wilson, Greville-Street, Hatton-Garden.

41.8 x 31.6 cm. Pp. i + 151 with 23 plates by T.C. Hofland (READING UNIV). There are variations in the sizes of this book, one BL is 40.5 x 31.7 cm., and SHEFFIELD is 43 x 32 cm. There are also variations between copies with hand-coloured illustrations to Numbers 1-3 and 18-22 (READING UNIV) and those without coloured illustrations. Copies have been rebound in various styles.

[BL 3 copies, READING UNIV 3 copies, SHEFFIELD]

A letter from T.C. Hofland to Sir John Soane, dated 13 June 1818, indicates that 150 copies were to be published in August at five guineas, and that the Hoflands were to be given 50 copies (SOANE). But Hofland wrote to Sir John on 10 April 1819, saying that the work on Whiteknights would be completed within about two months (SOANE). It must have been difficult for the Hoflands to sell the book after the Duke's financial crash, and *Fourteen Views of the Mansion and Garden Seats of White-Knights* (READING UNIV) was published by T.C. Hofland from 23 Newman Street, London, some time between 1822 and 1832, using some of the same engravings as are in the 1819 volume but without Mrs Hofland's commentary or poem; as late as 1846 Hofland's engravings of Whiteknights were still for sale under the title *Specimens of Garden Decorations and Oriental Scenery, Appropriate to Pleasure Grounds* (READING LIB).

1820

26   A LETTER OF AN ENGLISHWOMAN, 1820

The Gentleman's Magazine (Vol. 23, January 1845, p 101) says that this remonstrance by Mrs Hofland dealt with the unhappy differences between George IV and Queen Caroline, presumably during the time of the Inquiry by the House of Lords in 1820 into the Queen's conduct. The letter apparently urged the public not to believe that the Queen was innocent, merely because they disliked the King. Mary Mitford described the pamphlet as 'a letter to Hannah More from an English woman on the present crisis', and praised it warmly. *(The Life of Mary Russell Mitford, related in a selection from her letters to her friends,* the Revd A.G. L'Estrange, 3 volumes, London, 1870, II, p 111.). But though numerous other pamphlets on this great controversy do survive, Mrs Hofland's contribution has not yet come to light.

27   TALES OF THE PRIORY. By Mrs. Hofland | Quotation from Crabbe's *Preface* | In Four Volumes. Vol. I. London: Printed for Longman, Hurst, Rees, Orme, and Brown, Paternoster-Row. 1820.

17.2 × 10.2 cm. Printed by A. and R. Spottiswoode, Printers-Street, London. Pp. 298 + 2pp. advertising 'Popular Novels published by Longman, Hurst, Rees, Orme, and Brown, Paternoster-Row,' - Vol. I; Pp. 317 + 2 pp. advertising 'Popular Novels published by Longman, Hurst, Rees, Orme, and Brown, Paternoster-Row,' - Vol. II; Pp. 361 + 2 pp. advertising 'Popular

Novels published by Longman, Hurst, Rees, Orme, and Brown, Paternoster-Row,' - Vol. III; Pp. 309 - Vol. IV. BOD copy has four volumes rebound as two in library binding, BL rebound as one volume, lacking adverts; SHEFFIELD has all four volumes bound separately but lacking adverts in modern library binding c.1926.

[BL, BOD, SHEFFIELD]

Part of Vol. III (pp 207-261) and the whole of Vol. IV consist of 'Elizabeth and her Boys; or, the Beggar's Story', which Mrs. Hofland was to retell as a children's story later (see No. 50 below). The Longman Archive reveals that 750 copies were published in May 1820, and *NUC* records a New York edition the same year.

1821

28 THEODORE, or the Crusaders, a Tale for Youth. By Mrs. Hoffland, (sic), Author of "The Son of a Genius," and other Works for Young People | 3 lines from Shakespeare | vignette of knight on charger | London: John Harris and Son, St. Pauls Church Yard. (n.d.)

16.1 × 9.7 cm. Printed by H. Bryer, Bridge-street, Blackfriars, London. 24 illustrations engraved two to a page, two dated August 20th, 1821. Pp vi + Pp 184. Printed paper boards with abbreviated title-page on front, THEODORE, or the Crusaders, by Mrs. Hoffland | vignette of mounted knight fighting mounted Saracen | London: J. Harris and Son, Corner of St. Paul's Church Yard. On back, circular emblem of 'Harris and Son's Original Juvenile Library,' enclosing vignette of St. Paul's. Red roan, gilt lettering on spine of title *The Crusaders*.

[BL, BOD]

Though *CBEL* dates the first edition 1815, no copy of that date is known, and the gap between that date and the reprinting of what was evidently a popular work, with the clear indication of subsequent editions, suggests that MOON and RUSSELL are right in choosing 1821 as the date of the first edition, on the authority of *The English Catalogue of Books 1801-1836* and the fact that two of the book's plates are clearly dated 20 August 1821. (The Bodleian copy also carries an inscription dated Dec. 28th 1821).

72 Barbara Hofland

MOON cites seven editions by Harris: 1821, 1823, 1824, 1826, 1828, 1833 and 1838, and *NUC* records two American editions: Boston 1824, and New York 1886. The *CBEL* notes an edition of 1879, and the last known English appearance seems to be as No. XII in 'The Favourite Library', published by Griffith & Farran, which has advertisements dated 1886 (BELL).

1822

29   ALICIA AND HER AUNT; or, Think before you Speak. A Tale for young persons | 4 lines by Cowper | London: Printed for A.K. Newman and Co. Leadenhall-Street. 1822.

13.3 × 8 cm. Printed by J. Darling, Leadenhall-street, London. Engraved frontispiece and engraved abbreviated t.p. ALICIA AND HER AUNT, or Think before you Speak. A tale for young persons | vignette of old lady addressing two children | with explanation 'Mrs. Launceston with Edward & Charles' | London. Printed for A.K. Newman & Co. Leadenhall Street. 1822. Pp 171. SHEFFIELD in modern library binding c.1926.

[SHEFFIELD]

This precedes the 1841 (revised) edition cited by *CBEL*. *NUC* records editions in New York (1830) and Boston (1865 and 1868); the book was advertised in 'The Hofland Library' in the 1850s. The last known English edition seems to be that cited by *CBEL* for 1860 (?), though the book was still being advertised in the 1866 edition of *The Clergyman's Widow* by Nelson (BOD).

30   TALES OF THE MANOR. By Mrs. Hofland. | Quotation from Cervantes | In Four Volumes. Vol. I. London. Printed for Longman, Hurst, Rees, Orme, and Brown, Paternoster-Row. 1822.

15.6 × 8.6 cm. Pp 344 - Vol. I; Pp 309 - Vol II; Pp 342 + 6 pp advertising 'Popular Novels, published by Longman, Hurst, Rees, Orme, and Brown, Paternoster-Row,'- Vol. III: Pp 309 + 2 pp advertising 'Popular Novels, published by Longman, Hurst, Rees, Orme and Brown, Paternoster-Row,' - Vol. IV. BL has four volumes rebound as two in contemporary binding and lacks adverts; BOD has four volumes rebound as one. SHEFFIELD lacks volume I, and is rebound in modern library binding.

[BL, BOD, SHEFFIELD]

The Longman Archive shows that 500 copies were published in May 1822, and *NUC* records a New York edition, also of 1822.

1823

31   ADELAIDE; or, the Intrepid Daughter: a Tale, including historical anecdotes of Henry the Great and the Massacre of St. Bartholomew. By the Author of "Theodore", "Son of Genius", &c. | vignette of figure on white horse | London: J. Harris and Son, Corner of St. Paul's Church-Yard. 1823.

16.7 × 10 cm. Printed by S. and R. Bentley. 24 half-page engravings printed two to a page on 12 pages, dated March 30, 1823. Pp. vii (including Dedication dated Nov. 28th, 1822 p. vii) + 156 + 4 pp. advertising 'New and Useful Books for Young People, Published by Harris and Son.' Printed paper boards, on front abbreviated t.p. ADELAIDE; or, the Intrepid Daughter. Vignette of figure on white horse. By Mrs. Hofland. London. J. Harris and Son. MDCCCXXIII. On back, circular emblem of 'John Harris and Son's Original Juvenile Library', enclosing vignette of St. Paul's. Red roan spine with gilt lettering of title *Adelaide*.

[AC, READING UNIV]

MOON cites a second edition in 1825, third n.d., and fourth, 1830, while *NUC* records a fifth edition published by Newman in 1830 (?) and a Boston edition of 1834. The book was advertised as part of 'The Hofland Library' in the 1850s, and Mrs Moon remembers reading a copy as a child in the early years of this century!

32   THE DAUGHTER OF A GENIUS; a tale for Youth. By Mrs. Hoffland (sic), Author of "The Son of a Genius", "Ellen the Teacher", &c. &c. | 4 lines quoted from *Boarding School Recollections* | London: John Harris and Son, St. Paul's Church Yard. 1823.

16.3 × 9.5 cm. Printed by H. Bryer, Bridge-Street, Blackfriars, London. Engraved frontispiece pubd. Jany. 20. 1823 by Harris & Son Corner of St. Pauls. Pp iv (including Dedication dated Jany 10 p. iv) + Pp 197 + 2 pp advertising 'Works Written by the Same Author, and Published by J. Harris and

Son.' Paper boards with abbreviated t.p. - THE DAUGHTER OF A GENIUS: a tale for youth. By Mrs. Hoffland (sic), Author of "The Son of a Genius", "Ellen the Teacher", &c. &c. London: John Harris and Son. Corner of St. Paul's Church-Yard. MDCCCXXIII. On back board, circular emblem of 'Harris & Son's Original Juvenile Library' enclosing vignette of St. Paul's. Red roan spine, gilt lettering of title *Daughter of Genius*.

[READING UNIV]

In addition to the six Harris editions described by MOON (twice in 1823, 1826, 1828, 1832 and 1837), *NUC* also records editions in Boston (1824, 185? and 1865) and New York (1853 and 1886). *BIB* records an edition in Paris in 1829. Later English editions include a 'New Edition' published by Grant and Griffith in 1848 (RENIER), and its appearance as Volume X in 'The Favourite Library' published by Griffith and Farran, dated by catalogue 1879 (BOD), and a 'New Edition' of 1886 (*EC*, vol. ix).

33 INTEGRITY. A tale. By Mrs. Hofland, author of Tales of the Priory, Tales of the Manor, and a Son of Genius, &c. &c. | Quotation from Job | London: Printed for Longman, Hurst, Rees, Orme, and Brown, Paternoster-Row. 1823.

16.1 × 9.5 cm. Printed by A. & R. Spottiswoode, New-Street-Square, London. Engraved frontispiece, T. Stothard R.A. del., J.G. Walker sc. published by Longman, Hurst & Co. Paternoster Row April 15th 1823. Pp 264. BL bound with *Decision* (1824) in marbled boards, SHEFFIELD rebound in modern library binding c.1926.

[BL, SHEFFIELD]

The Longman Archive shows the first edition of 1,000 copies was published in April 1823, a second of 750 in 1824, and third of 1,000 in 1826. *CBEL* records editions in 1836 and 1840, and the book was advertised in 'The Hofland Library' in the 1850s. *NUC* records editions at Philadelphia in 1823 and 1828, and at Boston in 1849. After the Nelson edition of 1865 cited by *EC* (vol. ii), and the edition of 1868 cited by *CBEL*, the most recent English edition appears to have been a Nelson edition of 1871 (RENIER).

1824

34 PATIENCE. A tale. By Mrs. Hofland, author of Integrity, a tale; the Son of a Genius, Tales of the Priory, Tales of the Manor, &c. &c. | Quotation from St. Paul | London: Printed for Longman, Hurst, Rees, Orme, Brown, and Green. Paternoster-Row. 1824.

16.3 × 9.4 cm. Stereotyped and printed by J. and R. Childs, Bungay. Engraved frontispiece J. Hayter delt., J.G. Walker sc., published by Longman, Hurst & Co. Paternoster Row, Jany. 1824. Pp. 298. BL and SHEFFIELD both rebound in marbled boards.

[BL, SHEFFIELD]

The Longman Archive shows that after a first printing of 1,000 copies in January 1824, Longman reprinted the book in 1825 (500), 1827 (500) and 1833 (250). *NUC* only records one New York edition of 1825, but the book was republished in England in 1838, according to *CBEL*, and advertised in 'The Hofland Library' in the 1850s.

35 DECISION. A tale. By Mrs. Hofland, author of Integrity a tale, Patience a tale, the Son of a Genius; Tales of the Priory; Tales of the Manor, &c. &c. | "First know thy principles are just, and then be thou inflexible in the path of them." | London: Printed for Longman, Hurst, Rees, Orme, Brown, and Green, Paternoster-Row. 1824.

15.6 × 8.7 cm. Stereotyped and printed by J. and R. Childs, Bungay. Engraved frontispiece, H. Corbould delt., E. Finden sc., published by Longman, Hurst & Co., Paternoster Row, Novr. 8, 1824. Pp 272. BL rebound with *Integrity* of 1823 in marbled boards (see entry No. 33) SHEFFIELD rebound in modern library binding c.1926.

[BL, SHEFFIELD]

The Longman Archive shows that this book was published in November 1824 in an edition of 1,000 copies, and reprinted by them in 1825 (500), 1829 (250) and 1833 (250). It was subsequently reprinted in England both by Newman in 1835 (RENIER) and in 'The Hofland Library' of the 1850s. *NUC* records editions in Boston (1848) and New York (1825 and 1867), and later English editions include those published by Nelson in 1865, (*EC*, vol.ii), Nelson in 1870 (AC), 1867 (RENIER), and 1873 (*EC*, vol.iii).

1825

36 ALFRED CAMPBELL, THE YOUNG PILGRIM; containing travels in Egypt and the Holy Land. With twenty-four engravings. By Mrs. Hofland, author of "Son of a Genius" &c. &c. | "Let us go to Jerusalem" | vignette of pilgrims praying before shrine | London: John Harris, Corner of St. Paul's Church-Yard. 1825.

16.7 × 10 cm. Printed by Cox and Bayliss, Great Queen Street, London. Twenty-four engravings printed two to a page, published 6 April 1825, by J. Harris, St. Paul's Church Yd. Pp viii + 230. Paper boards. On front, ALFRED CAMPBELL, THE YOUNG PILGRIM; containing travels in Egypt and the Holy Land | vignette of pilgrims praying before shrine | London: John Harris, Corner of St. Paul's Church-Yard. On back, circular emblem of helmeted lady. Red roan spine with gilt lettering *Alfred Campbell*.

[BL, SHEFFIELD]

The engravings dated April 6th, 1825, suggest that the book was published early in the year, and MOON only records a second edition of 1826, but 'a new edition, with additions' was published by Newman in 1841 (BL), and *NUC* also records an undated Boston edition. The book was also advertised in 'The Hofland Library' of the 1850s.

37 MODERATION. A tale. By Mrs. Hofland, Author of Integrity a Tale, Patience a Tale, Decision a Tale, The Son of a Genius; Tales of the Priory; Tales of the Manor, &c. | Quotation from St. Paul | London: Printed for Longman, Hurst, Rees, Orme, Brown, and Green, Paternoster-Row. 1825.

16.5 × 9.5 cm. Stereotyped and printed by J. and R. Childs, Bungay. Engraved frontispiece J.M. Wright delt., T.S. Engleheart sculpt., dated Augt. 1825. Pp. 252. Both BL and BOD rebound, the former with first edition of *Reflection* of 1826 - see entry No. 38.

[BL, BOD]

The Longman Archive shows that an edition of 1,000 copies was published in June 1825, and another of 750 in 1826. *NUC* records editions both in Philadelphia (1826) and Boston (1860?), and the book was advertised in 'The Hofland Library' of the 1850s. The last English edition seems to have been a 'new edition' by Hall and Virtue dated by the label 1865 (RENIER).

1826

38 REFLECTION. A tale. By Mrs. Hofland, Author of Integrity, a tale; Patience, a tale; Decision, a tale; Moderation, a tale; The Son of a Genius; Tales of the Priory; Tales of the Manor, &c. &c. | 1 line from Shakespeare | London: Printed for Longman, Rees, Orme, Brown, and Green, Paternoster-Row. 1826.

16.2 × 9.4 cm. Printed by J. and R. Childs, Bungay. Engraved frontispiece J.M. Wright delt., Mitchell sculpt. Published Longman, Rees & Co. Paternoster-Row, June 1826. Pp 267. BL, BOD and SHEFFIELD all rebound, BL with *Moderation* of 1825.

[BL, BOD, SHEFFIELD]

The Longman Archive shows that, after a first edition of 1,000 copies in June 1826, Longman published a second edition of 249 copies in 1831. *NUC* records editions by Newman in 1834 and 1835, and American editions in Boston in 1845, 1848, 1849 and 1851. *CBEL* records a later English edition of 1838; the book was advertised in 'The Hofland Library' of the 1850s, and later English editions include one cited by the *CBEL* of 1868, and Nelson editions of 1865 and 1873 (*EC*, vols. ii and iii).

39 WILLIAM AND HIS UNCLE BEN. A tale. Designed for the use of young people. Prepared for the press by Mrs. Hofland, author of the Merchant's Widow and family; Clergyman's Widow and family; the Daughter-in-Law; the Barbadoes Girl; Affectionate Brothers; Panorama of Europe; Young Northern Traveller; &c. | 4 lines by Crabbe | London: Printed for A.K. Newman and Co., Leadenhall-Street, 1826.

13.8 × 8.5 cm. Printed by J. Darling, Leadenhall-Street, London. Engraved frontispiece, E. Burney Del, S. Springsguth Sculp. Engraved abbreviated t.p.

WILLIAM AND HIS UNCLE BEN A tale designed for the use of young people. Prepared for the press by Mrs. Hofland. Author of the Clergyman's Widow &c. &c. London, printed for A.K. Newman & Co. Leadenhall Street. Pp 149 + 3 pp advertising 'Publications for the Instruction and Amusement of Youth, sold by A.K. Newman & Co. Leadenhall Street.' BL marbled boards, red roan spine with gold bands, and title in gilt *William and his Uncle Ben*. SHEFFIELD rebound in modern library binding.

[BL, SHEFFIELD]

The book was reprinted by Newman in 1829 (RENIER); GUMUCHIAN records an edition of c.1835 and the book was advertised in 'The Hofland Library' of the 1850s. *NUC* records an edition of 1865. In addition to the edition of 1865 cited by *CBEL*, the most recent English edition seems to be one by Nelson of 1865 (?) cited by *EC* (vol.ii) and in the Author's collection.

40   THE YOUNG PILGRIM, or Alfred Campbell's Return to the East. And his travels in Egypt, Nubia, Asia Minor, Arabia Petraea, &c. &c. By Mrs. Hofland, Author of "Alfred Campbell, or the Young Pilgrim", "The Son of a Genius", &c. &c. (Quotation from Numbers XX). London: John Harris, Corner of St. Paul's Church-Yard, MDCCCXXVI.

16.5 × 10 cm. Printed by S. and R. Bentley. 12 half-page engravings printed two to a page, dated May 1, 1826. Pp xii + 211 + 2 pp. advertising 'Harris's Books for Young People.' AC has marbled boards, red roan spine, gilt lettering on spine *The Young Pilgrim*, SHEFFIELD rebound.

[AC, SHEFFIELD]

MOON records two other printings by Harris up to 1830, and the book was published by Newman in 1840 and 1841 (RENIER), and advertised in 'The Hofland Library' in the 1850s. *NUC* records one American edition only: New York in 1828.

1827

41   SELF-DENIAL. A tale. By Mrs. Hofland, author of Integrity, a tale; Patience, a tale; Decision, a tale; Moderation, a tale; Reflection, a tale; the Son of a Genius; Tales of the Priory; Tales of the Manor; &c. &c. | "Let him deny

himself" | London: Printed for Longman, Rees, Orme, Brown, and Green, Paternoster-Row. 1827.

17 x 10.6 cm. Printed by J. and R. Childs, Bungay. Engraved frontispiece, J.M. Wright delt, T.S. Engleheart sculpt. Pubd. by Longman & Co. London, Octr. 1827. Pp 254. BL and SHEFFIELD both rebound in modern library binding.

[BL, SHEFFIELD]

The Longman Archive shows that after a first edition of 750 copies in June 1827, they republished the book in an edition of 250 copies in 1830, before selling Mrs Hofland's works to A.K. Newman, who republished this tale in 1834 (BELL), 1835 and 1836 (RENIER) and 1846 (AC). *NUC* records editions in New York in 1828 and Boston in 1845, and the book was still being advertised as part of 'The Hofland Library' in the 1850s.

1828

42 THE YOUNG CADET; or Henry Delamere's Voyage to India, his travels in Hindostan, his account of the Burmese War, and the wonders of Elora. By Mrs. Hofland, Author of "The Son of a Genius", "Daughter of a Genius", "Alfred Campbell, The Young Pilgrim", "Theodore", &c. &c. | 4 lines by Shakespeare | London: John Harris, Corner of St. Paul's Church-Yard. (n.d.)

16.8 x 10.2 cm. Printed by S. and R. Bentley, Dorset Street, London. 12 half-page engravings printed two to a page including frontispiece. Pubd. Decr. 1827 by J. Harris, Corner of St. Paul's. Pp. xi (including Dedication dated Nov. 1, 1827 p. iv) + 232. READING UNIV has 2 pp advertising 'Harris's Books for Young People'. Printed paper boards with abbreviated t.p. THE YOUNG CADET; or travels in Hindostan. By Mrs. Hofland | vignette of Indian smoking hookah pipe | 4 lines by Shakespeare | London: John Harris, Corner of St. Paul's Church Yard. On back, circular emblem containing inscription 'John Harris. St. Paul's Church Yard' and helmeted woman's head. Roan spine, gilt lettering *The Young Cadet*.

[AC, READING UNIV]

Though *CBEL* cites an edition of 1821, no copy of that date is known; the dating of the *Dedicatory letter* of November 1st, 1827, with the frontispiece engraving also dated 1827, suggests that this copy of 1827 is the first edition, a suggestion supported by *The English Catalogue of Books 1801-1836*.

MOON cites a second edition of c.1830, and the *CBEL* a revised edition of 1836. *BIB* notes a French translation in Paris of 1830. *NUC* records editions in New York (1828), Boston (1829), and Philadelphia (1831), and the book was also advertised in 'The Hofland Library' in the 1850s.

43 AFRICA DESCRIBED in its ancient and present state; including accounts from Bruce, Ledyard, Lucas, Horneman, Park, Salt, Jackson, Sir F. Henniker, Belzoni, the Portuguese Missionaries, and Others, Down to the Recent Discoveries by Major Denham, Dr. Oudney, and Captain Clapperton. Intended for the Use of Young Persons and Schools. By Mrs. Hofland. London: Printed for Longman, Rees, Orme, Brown, and Green, Paternoster-Row. 1828.

18.5 × 10.7 cm. Printed by A. & R. Spottiswoode, New-Street-Square. 12 pp advertising 'New Works, Printed for Longman, Rees, Orme, Brown, & Green, London' dated March 1828. Folded Map published 1823 by A. Constable & Co. Edinburgh, and Longman and Compy. London. Engraved by Thomson & Hall. Pp viii + 291. Boards with label on spine *Africa Described* by Mrs. Hofland 6s. 6d.

[READING UNIV]

This is a general account of the continent, including Egypt, Nubia and Abyssinia, and with a retelling of the travels of such men as Mungo Park and the Portuguese missionaries.
    The Longman Archive shows that a first edition of 1,000 copies was published in December 1827, and *CBEL* records another edition in 1834.

44 KATHERINE. A tale. | Quotation from *The Second Maiden's Tragedy* | In Four Volumes. Vol. I. London: A.K. Newman & Co. Leadenhall-Street, 1828.

17.5 × 10 cm. Printed by J. Darling, Leadenhall-Street, London. Pp 247 [+ 1 advertising 'New Publications'] | - Vol. I; Pp. 230 (+ 1 advertising 'New Publications') - Vol. II; Pp. 234 - Vol. III; Pp 240 - Vol. IV. BL and BOD both have four volumes rebound as one.

[BL, BOD]

Mrs Hofland's name is missing from the title-page of this novel, and although it is normally attributed to her, for example, by both *CBEL* and H & L, there is some doubt.

The story of a Cumberland clergyman's daughter, and the vicissitudes of her love affairs after her mother's death, happily resolved by her marriage to her first lover, is typically Mrs Hofland; Newman was one of her most regular publishers. But the book neither bears Mrs Hofland's name nor references to her other works on the title-page, and is not ascribed to her by RAMSAY. None of these factors individually is absolutely crucial, for RAMSAY omits several of her other books from his *Life* (for example, *Ivanowna*), and Newman might have wished to publish the romance without revealing that its author was also a children's writer. But the current revisers of Halkett and Laing are not able to provide evidence for the earlier editors' attribution to Mrs Hofland (op.cit., Vol III, p. 214), and the use of epigraphs and chapter-headings, drawn from such authors and texts as Chaucer, George Withers, Sir Henry Wotton and *The Second Maiden's Tragedy*, is quite unlike Mrs Hofland's normal practice.

45(a)   TALES OF CLAIRMONT CASTLE: containing the Woodville Family; the Franks; and Sir Francis Vanhesan. Prepared for the Press by Mrs. Hofland, author of the Clergyman's Widow, Merchant's Widow, Good Grandmother, Daughter in Law, &c. London: Published by A.K. Newman & Co. 1828.

12.8 × 7.7 cm. Printed by Dean and Munday, Threadneedle-Street. Engraved frontispiece drawn by Fussell, engraved by W. Evans (?), published by Dean and Munday, Threadneedle Street, Oct. 1828. Pp 140 + 3 pp. advertising 'Juvenile Works published by A.K. Newman & Co. Leadenhall-Street.' including *Tales of Clairmont Castle*; second series; containing the Pedigree, the Spring Gun, and the Fugitive: with beautiful frontispiece. SHEFFIELD copy in modern library binding c.1926.

[SHEFFIELD]

45(b)   TALES OF CLAIRMONT CASTLE; second series; containing the Pedigree, the Spring Gun, and the Fugitive. With frontispiece.

No known copy of this edition survives, but *OSB* records a copy of the 'Second

Series', c.1830, containing the White Lie; the Pedigree; the Spring Gun; and the Fugitive. Prepared for the Press by Mrs. Hofland. Pp 140.

Both books of Tales are frequently advertised in other Newman publications of the 1830s, and *NUC* records a Philadelphian edition containing both series in 18--, a copy of which is in AC.

(BL and GUMUCHIAN also record a copy of *A Few Weeks at Clairmont Castle* by Miss Pearson of 1828, which contains the same four tales as the volume of the Second Series, so it is possible that Mrs Hofland revised these for republication later).

1829

46   THE YOUNG CRUSOE, or the Shipwrecked Boy.   Containing an Account of his Shipwreck, and Residence for several months alone, upon an uninhabited island.   By Mrs. Hofland, Author of the Clergyman's Widow; Merchant's Widow; Sisters; Good Grandmother; Affectionate Brothers; Panorama of Europe; Daughter-in-Law; Barbadoes Girl; Blind Farmer; &c. &c. London: Printed for A.K. Newman and Co. 1829.

14 x 8.5 cm. Printed by J. Darling, Leadenhall Street. Engraved frontispiece E. Burney Del, S. Springsguth. Sculp. Engraved abbreviated t.p. THE YOUNG CRUSOE, or the Shipwrecked Boy. By Mrs. Hofland. Author of the Clergyman's Widow, Merchant's Widow, Sisters, Good Grandmother, Affectionate Brothers, Panorama of Europe, Daughter in Law, Barbadoes Girl, Blind Farmer, Young Northern Traveller, &c. &c. London. Printed for A.K. Newman & Co. Pp 195 (+1 advertising 'New Publications for the Instruction and Amusement of Youth, sold by A.K. Newman and Co. London.') Marbled boards, red roan spine, with gilt lettering of title *Young Crusoe*.

[READING UNIV]

The *CBEL* entry is both sparse and inaccurate, misdating the first and recording only one other edition, for this was Mrs. Hofland's most enduring success. Though the READING UNIV copy is apparently the first edition and clearly dated 1829, the book seems to have been published with that date in December 1828 - a common publisher's device to catch the Christmas trade - for *The Athenaeum* (No. 60, 17 December 1828) lists it among books published during the week (i.e. between 10 and 17 December) on page 957. The second edition of *The Good Grandmother* (1828) also advertises it under 'New Publications' of 1828. GUMUCHIAN records a Newman edition c.1830 and RENIER contains editions by Newman (for 1836?) and Nelson (1874, 1876, 1879 and 1881), while *EC* (vols ii and iii) record further Nelson editions in 1866 and 1882, and READING UNIV has a Nelson edition of 1886. *NUC* records publications in New York in 1833, 1859 and 1878, and the book was also advertised in 'The Hofland Library'of the 1850s.

The last known English edition of this work is: *The Young Crusoe* .... edited by Alfonzo Gardiner. Published by John Heywood, Manchester, n.d. but with a Preface dated 1894.

[SHEFFIELD]

47 BEATRICE, a tale founded on facts. By Mrs. Hofland | 4 lines by Shakespeare | In Three Volumes. Vol. I. London: Printed for Longman, Rees, Orme, Brown, and Green, Paternoster-Row, 1829.

17.5 × 10 cm. Printed by A. and R. Spottiswoode, New-Street-Square, London. Pp 324 + pp iii advertising 'Works recently Published by Longman, Rees, Orme, Brown, and Green, Paternoster-Row' - Vol. I; Pp 354 - Vol. II; Pp 312 - Vol. III. ABER and SHEFFIELD both have three volumes rebound separately in library binding, though ABER lacks adverts. BL and BOD three volumes rebound in library binding as one volume, BL lacking adverts.

[ABER, BL, BOD, SHEFFIELD]

The Longman Archive shows that 500 copies were published in July 1829, and *NUC* records one American edition in New York (1830).

1830

48 THE STOLEN BOY. A story, founded on facts. By Mrs. Hofland, Author of the Clergyman's Widow; the Sisters; Blind Farmer; Barbadoes Girl; Panorama of Europe; Young Crusoe; Young Northern Traveller; Good Grandmother; Affectionate Brothers; Daughter-in-Law; Merchant's Widow; &c. &c. | prose quotation from Shakespeare | London: Printed for A.K. Newman and Co.

14.5 × 8.6 cm. Printed by J. Darling, Leadenhall Street. Engraved frontispiece E. Burney Del, Engraved on Steel by S. Springsguth. Engraved abbreviated t.p.

THE STOLEN BOY. An Indian Tale. by Mrs. Hofland Author of The Clergyman's Widow. Merchant's Widow. Sisters. Good Grandmother. Affectionate Brothers. Panorama of Europe. Daughter in Law. Barbadoes Girl. Blind Farmer. Young Crusoe. Young Northern Traveller. &c. &c. London. Printed for A.K. Newman & Co. Pp vii (including 'To the Reader' stating that the story was first published in the *Juvenile Souvenir* for 1828 p[v]) + 168 + 2pp advertising 'New Publications for the Instruction & Amusement of Youth, sold by A.K. Newman and Co. London,' with *The Stolen Boy* advertised for 1830 at 2s. 6d. AC paper boards, red roan spine, with *Stolen Boy* in gilt. BL rebound with THE ADVENTURES OF ARISTON by an Eton Boy, London, 1830. SHEFFIELD rebound in modern library binding.

[AC, BL, SHEFFIELD]

'To the Reader', p (v) says the story was published in the *Juvenile Souvenir* for 1828, and A. Boyle (*An Index to the Annuals*, Worcester, 1967) also records it in *New Year's Gift*.

This book, which its list of 'New Publications' helps to date 1830, was reprinted by Newman n.d. (RENIER), and appeared in 'The Hofland Library' of the 1850s. Perhaps because of its American setting, it seems to have enjoyed even wider popularity overseas. *NUC* records American editions, sometimes under the title of *Little Manuel or The Captive Boy* in New York (1830), Boston (1831?) and Cincinnati (1844), as well as the following European editions:
Manuel o el Nino Robada, Paris, 1836
Der gersubte Knabe, Reutlingen, 1842
Manoel, aventures d'une jeune Espagnol, Rouen, 1852.

BIB notes the last and eight other editions, in Paris in 18--, 1835, and 1862, in Rouen in 1854, 1859 and 1865, and in Lille in 1862 and 1863.

1832

49 POETICAL ILLUSTRATIONS OF THE VARIOUS SCENES REPRESENTED IN MR. LINTON'S "SKETCHES IN ITALY." By Mrs. Hofland. London: Printed by Frederic Shoberl, Jun. Long Acre, 1832.

27.3 × 21.4 cm. Pp ii + 32. Paper wrappers, the front identical with t.p., on the back extracts from 'Notices of "Sketches in Italy," by W. Linton' from *The Metropolitan, The Library of the Fine Arts, The New Monthly and London Magazine, The London Literary Gazette*, and *The Morning Post*.

[SOANE]

A poem in blank verse describing Rome, Sorrento and other places, illustrated by W. Linton's *Sketches in Italy*, published separately in 1832.

50   RICHMOND, AND ITS SURROUNDING SCENERY. Engraved by and under the direction of W.B. Cooke. With descriptive letterpress, by Mrs. Hofland. Dedicated, by permission, to Her Grace the Duchess of Northumberland. Containing twenty-four plates. London: W.B. Cooke, 27, Charlotte Street, Bloomsbury. 1832.

27.7 × 20.4 cm. Printed by C. Whittingham, Chiswick Press. Pp x (including Dedication to the Duchess of Northumberland by Mrs. Hofland dated October 17th, 1832) + 24 plates (17 drawn by J.D. Harding, 6 by G. Barnard, and 1 by Frederick Smith, engraved either by W.B. Cooke or Frederick Smith, and dated either June 1, 1831, or June 1, 1832.) + Pp 74. Both BL and SHEFFIELD rebound, the latter in modern library binding c.1926.

[BL, SHEFFIELD]

1833

51   ELIZABETH, AND HER THREE BEGGAR BOYS. By Mrs. Hofland, author of the Clergyman's Widow; Good Grandmother; Stolen Boy; Daughter-in-Law; Merchant's Widow; Young Crusoe; Panorama of Europe; Blind Farmer; Sisters; Barbadoes Girl; Affectionate Brothers; Young Northern Traveller; &c. &c. London: A.K. Newman and Co. (n.d.)

13.9 × 8.8 cm. Printed by J. Darling, Leadenhall Street, London, Verso front cover and f.e.p. bearing 2 pp. advertising 'Juvenile and Prize Books, printed for A.K. Newman and Co. London' (Adverts refer to *Rich Boys and Poor Boys* of 1833. See 52 below). Engraved frontispiece, E. Burney Del., Engraved in steel S. Springsguth. Engraved abbreviated t.p. ELIZABETH, AND HER THREE BEGGAR BOYS. By Mrs. Hofland, author of the Clergyman's Widow, &c. London: A.K. Newman & Co. Leadenhall Street. Pp iv (with note 'To the Reader' explaining that the story has been carefully abridged and was originally published, combined with similar productions, in a work of four volumes) + Pp 160. BL in marble boards with decorated leather spine bearing title *Hofland's Elizabeth*.   SHEFFIELD (13.8 × 8.1 cm) lacks t.p. and rebound in modern library binding.

[BL, SHEFFIELD]

Though RUSSELL cites *The English Catalogue of Books, 1801-1836* and the BL copy, in support of dating this 1832, both SHEFFIELD and BL copies contain an advertisement for *Rich Boys and Poor Boys,* which has a *Dedication* dated 1833, so that seems more likely for the dating of *Elizabeth.*

NUC records a New York edition of 1838, and the book appeared in 'The Hofland Library' in the 1850s, but the last known edition seems to be one by Nelson, which its label dates as 1867 (AC).

52 RICH BOYS AND POOR BOYS; and other tales. By Mrs. Hofland, Author of Elizabeth and her Three Beggar Boys; Panorama of Europe; Clergyman's Widow; Merchant's Widow; Blind Farmer; Barbadoes Girl; Affectionate Brothers; Sisters; Good Grandmother; William and his Uncle Ben; Young Northern Traveller; Young Crusoe; Daughter-in-Law; Stolen Boy, &c. &c. | Quotation from *Proverbs* | London: Printed for A.K. Newman and Co. (n.d.)

14 × 8.7 cm. Printed by J. Darling, Leadenhall-Street, London. Engraved frontispiece J. Williams Del. Engraved in Steel by Springsguth. Engraved abbreviated t.p. RICH BOYS AND POOR BOYS, and other tales. By Mrs. Hofland, Author of the Clergyman's Widow &c. London. A.K. Newman & Co. Leadenhall Street. Pp ii (including Dedication dated April 3, 1833 p ii) + 171. Verso front cover and f.e.p. bear pp 2 advertising 'Juvenile Books, printed for A.K. Newman and Co. London' BL marbled boards, red roan spine with gilt floral decorations and gilt title *Rich Boys & Poor Boys.* READING UNIV marbled boards but new spine.

[BL, READING UNIV]

The stories, 'Rich Boys and Poor Boys' (*Juvenile Forget-me-not*), 'The Passionate Little Girl' (*New Year's Gift*), 'William and his Story Books' (Ackermann's *Juvenile Forget-me-not*), and 'The Riding School' (Ackermann's *Juvenile Forget-me-not*), all appeared in Annuals before being published together in one collection.

The book's Dedication of April 3, 1833, helps to date this book, pp. (iii)-v. SHEFFIELD possesses a 'New Edition', published by Hall and Virtue soon after this, and *CBEL* cites editions of 1836 (?) and 1840. 'The Hofland Library' advertised an edition in the 1850s, and *NUC* records a Boston edition of 1836.

1834

53 THE CAPTIVES IN INDIA, a tale; and A WIDOW AND A WILL. By Mrs. Hofland. In Three Volumes. Vol. I. London: Richard Bentley, New Burlington Street. (Successor to Henry Colburn) 1834.

18.6 × 11.1 cm. Printed by Samuel Bentley, Dorset Street, Fleet Street, London. Pp i (an advert dated August 1832) + Pp 327 - Vol. I; Pp 320 - Vol. II; Pp 338 - Vol. III. BL has three volumes rebound separately in modern library binding, BOD three volumes rebound as one in library binding.

[BL, BOD]

The Captives in India runs to p 235 of Volume III, and *A Widow and a Will* from p (239) to 338.

NUC records an edition in Washington in 1835.

1835

54 DESCRIPTION OF THE HOUSE AND MUSEUM ON THE NORTH SIDE OF LINCOLN'S INN FIELDS, the residence of Sir John Soane, Professor of Architecture in the Royal Academy, one of the Architects attached to His Majesty's Office of Works, Architect to the Bank of England and College of Surgeons, F.R.S. R.A. F.S.A. Grand Superintendent of the works of the United Fraternity of Free and Accepted Masons of England, Membre Honoraire de L'Academie Imperiale et Royale des Beaux Arts en Vienne, Consigliere Corrispondente Della Ducale Accademia di Belle Arti, Parma. &c. &c. &c. With Graphic Illustrations and Incidental Details. London: Printed by Levey, Robson, and Franklyn, St. Martin's Lane. Not Published. Only One Hundred and Fifty Copies printed.

36.5 × 27 cm. Engraved frontispiece of Chantrey's bust of Soane, xxxviii engraved plates by various artists, and 11 engraved vignettes. Pp. xiv + Pp. 109. (SOANE also contains *Description de la Maison et du Musée* .... demeure du Chevalier Soane. (A French edition of the *Description*) Levey, Robson, et

Franklyn, St. Martin's Lane, Londres, with the 11 vignettes, but lacking the plates, Pp xiv + 103). Contemporary binding blind-stamped with 'Description of the House and the Museum of Sir John Soane' blocked in gilt on front, and 'Sir John Soane's House and Museum 1936' in gilt on spine. All edges gilt.

A *Dedication* by John Soane to the Duke of Sussex is dated September 10, 1835, and a note on the *List of Plates*, p x, records that additional prose descriptions were written by a lady distinguished by the initials B.H., and are found on Pp 4, 8, 11, 13, 23, 36, 44, 54, 81, and 90. (Barbara Hofland's notes actually appear on pp 4-5, 8-9, 11, 13-14, 23-25, 27-29, 36-40, 44-46, 47, 54-55, 81-82 and 90-98).

[SOANE]

In 1919 an abbreviated version of the *Description*, containing an introductory note about the Hoflands, was published: POPULAR DESCRIPTION OF SIR JOHN SOANE'S HOUSE, MUSEUM & LIBRARY written in 1835 by Mrs. Barbara Hofland Authoress of 'A Son of Genius,' &c. Edited from the 'Description' of 1835 by Sir John Soane, R.A. by Arthur T. Bolton, F.S.A., F.R.I.B.A. Soane Medallist, Curator of Sir John Soane's Museum. With eight illustrations of the House and Museum | Medallion of Sir John Soane 1753-1837 | Printed at Oxford by Frederick Hall, 1919.

18.5 × 12.4 cm. 8 illustrations. Pp 55 (+ 1 advertising 'Soane Museum Publications') Blue paper wrappers identical with t.p. but adding at foot 'Soane Museum Publications, No. 6. To Be Had Only At the Museum. All rights reserved. Price Sixpence.'

[BL, SHEFFIELD, SOANE]

55 FORTITUDE. A tale by Mrs. Hofland, author of Africa Described; Integrity; Decision; Patience; Moderation; Reflection; Self-Denial; Clergyman's Widow; &c. &c. | 2 lines by Crabbe | London: A.K. Newman and Company. 1835.

14.9 × 9.1 cm. Printed by J. Darling, Leadenhall Street, London. Engraved frontispiece drawn by H. Richter, engraved by F. Bacon. Engraved abbreviated t.p. FORTITUDE. A tale. By Mrs. Hofland, author of Africa Described, Integrity, Decision, Patience, Moderation, Reflection, Self-Denial, Clergyman's

Widow, &c. &c. | 2 lines from Crabbe | London: A.K. Newman & Company. Pp 259 (+ 1 advertising 'Mrs. Hofland's Works') + 2 pp. advertising 'Juvenile and Prize Books, printed for A.K. Newman and Co. London.' BL rebound in marbled boards with all edges gilt, SHEFFIELD in modern binding c.1926.

[BL, SHEFFIELD]

A 'New Edition' also by Newman, appeared in 1838 (BELL), and the book was advertised in 'The Hofland Library' in the 1850s, but from now on Mrs Hofland's new books go through fewer editions.

1837

56 HUMILITY. A tale. By Mrs. Hofland, Author of Africa Described; Patience; Self-Denial; Moderation; Integrity; Fortitude; Decision; Reflection; Young Cadet; Clergyman's Widow; &c. | Quotations from the New Testament (1 Peter 5:5 and Ephesians 4:2) | London: A.K. Newman and Company. 1837.

15.8 x 9.6 cm. Printed by J. Darling, Leadenhall Street, London. Engraved frontispiece J.M. Wright and S. Springsguth on steel. Engraved abbreviated t.p. HUMILITY. A tale. By Mrs. Hofland Author of Africa Described, Decision, Fortitude, Integrity, Moderation, Patience, Reflection, Self Denial, Young Cadet, Clergyman's Widow, &c. &c. | "Be clothed in Humility" | London. A.K. Newman & Company. Pp 253 + 2 pp advertising 'Juvenile and Prize Books printed for A.K. Newman and Co. London.' SHEFFIELD copy in decorated and embossed boards, spine with gilt lettering *Hofland's Humility* all edges gilt. BL rebound in marbled boards.

[BL, SHEFFIELD]

The book was included in 'The Hofland Library' of the 1850s; *EC* (vol.ii) records a Nelson edition of 1865, and *CBEL* cites an edition of 1868.

1838

57 ENERGY. A tale. By Mrs. Hofland, Author of Africa Described; Fortitude; Moderation; Integrity; Decision; Reflection; Self-Denial; Young Cadet; Humility; Patience; Clergyman's Widow; &c. | Quotation from

Ecclesiastes | London: A.K. Newman and Company. 1838.

15.8 × 9.4 cm. Printed by Darling & Son, Leadenhall Street, London. Engraved Frontispiece S. Williams del., S. Springsguth. Stel. Engraved abbreviated t.p. ENERGY. A tale, by Mrs. Hofland. Author of Africa Described, Decision, Fortitude, Humility, Integrity, Moderation, Patience, Reflection, Self Denial, Young Cadet, Clergyman's Widow, &c. &c. | Quotation from Ecclesiastes | London, A.K. Newman & Company. Pp 282 + 4 pp advertising 'Juvenile and Prize Books' READING UNIV in embossed binding, spine with gilt lettering *Hofland's Energy*, all edges gilt, similar to 56 above. BELL, however, although similar to READING UNIV in all other respects, in red cloth boards with embossed design. On front and back oblong gold medallions of fronds with trumpet-shaped flowers, and gilt lettering on spine, *Energy by Mrs. Hofland,* and medallion design. All edges gilt. (BOD copy rebound). The existence of two different versions of the First Edition is puzzling. By the 1830s Newman seems to have been republishing many of Mrs Hofland's earlier books and some of her new titles in what his advertisement for 'Juvenile and Prize Books' called 'elegant embossed bindings, with gilt edges and lettered' priced at five shillings each. (*Energy* was included in this series.) Newman also advertised some of Mrs. Hofland's books, 'neatly half bound in roan' at two shillings and sixpence. BELL fits into neither of these categories. Either it is a maverick or, more likely, Newman published the red cloth at a lower price when sales of the embossed edition proved disappointing.

[BELL, BOD, READING UNIV]

SHEFFIELD has a later but undated Newman edition, and the book was advertised in 'The Hofland Library' of the 1850s. *NUC* records two Boston editions (18-- and 1844).

1839

58   THE ILLUSTRATED ALPHABET, with poetry by Mrs. Hofland, Author of "Patience," "Clergyman's Widow," &c. &c. London: A.K. Newman and Co., Leadenhall Street, 1839.

14.1 × 12.5 cm. Pp of text (28), each page having verso blank to make a total of pp. 56 + 2 pp advertising 'Juvenile and Prize Books, printed for A.K. Newman & Co. London' Green paper wrappers. On front, border design of stars surrounding THE ILLUSTRATED ALPHABET, with poetry, by Mrs. Hofland, author of "Patience," "Clergyman's Widow", &c. &c. London: A.K. Newman and Co., Leadenhall Street, 1839. Halne Brothers, Printers, Gracechurch Street. On back, blocked advertisement for 'Juvenile Books, printed for A.K. Newman and Co., London.' SHEFFIELD, which is rebound in modern library binding c. 1929, seems to be a variant, its t.p. 13.5 × 12 cm, and with Pp 58 but lacking the adverts.

[BL, SHEFFIELD]

1840

59 FAREWELL TALES. By Mrs. Hofland, Author of Africa Described; Energy; Moderation; Integrity; Decision; Reflection; Self-Denial; Young Cadet; Humility; Patience; Fortitude; Clergyman's Widow; &c. | 4 lines from an anonymous poem | London: A.K. Newman and Company, 1840.

15.9 × 9.7 cm. Printed by Darling & Son, 31 Leadenhall Street. Engraved frontispiece by S. Williams and S. Springsguth Stel (?), and engraved abbreviated t.p. FAREWELL TALES, by Mrs. Hofland. Author of Africa Described, Decision, Fortitude, Integrity, Moderation, Patience, Reflection, Self Denial, Young Cadet, Humility, Energy, Merchant's Widow, &c. London, A.K. Newman & Company. Pp iii (including Dedication dated January 28, 1839) + 262 + 3 pp advertising 'Mrs. Hofland's Works' and 'Juvenile Books Printed for A.K. Newman & Co. London'. BL and READING UNIV have embossed boards with gilt lettering on spine of *Hofland's Farewell Tales*, and with all edges gilt, SHEFFIELD rebound in modern library binding c.1926.

[BL, READING UNIV, SHEFFIELD]

A *Dedicatory letter* (pp (i)-iii) to Margaretta, the daughter of 'My Dear Friends, Mr. and Mrs. Ayrton' of Chester, offers her 'the last volume of tales I shall write ....'

NUC cites editions in Boston (184? and 1847) and New York (in 184?), and the book was also advertised as part of 'The Hofland Library' in the 1850s.

1842

60 THE CZARINA; an historical romance of the Court of Russia. By Mrs.

92 Barbara Hofland

Hofland, | 5 lines by Shakespeare | In Three Volumes. Vol I. London: Henry Colburn, Publisher, Great Marlborough Street. 1842.

19 × 11 cm. Printed by J. Shoberl, Jun., Rupert Street, Haymarket, London. Printer to H.R.H. Prince Albert. Pp. 302 + 2 pp advertising 'Interesting New Works, just published by Mr. Colburn,' - Vol. I; Pp 317 - Vol. II; Pp 325 - Vol. III. BL and BOD have three volumes rebound as one volume in library binding, SHEFFIELD three separate volumes.

[BL, BOD, SHEFFIELD]

NUC records a New York edition of 1842, and *The Gentleman's Magazine* (vol.23, 1845, p. 101) says 20,000 copies were sold in America on its first appearance, though the apparent absence of subsequent editions perhaps throws some doubt on that.

61 THE GODMOTHER'S TALES. By Mrs. Hofland, Author of Africa Described; Energy; Integrity; Farewell Tales; Decision; Reflection; Self-Denial; Young Cadet; Humility; Patience; Fortitude; Clergyman's Widow; Moderation; etc. London: A.K. Newman and Company. 1842.

13.3 × 10.5 cm. Printed by Darling & Son, 31, Leadenhall Street. Engraved frontispiece S. Williams. Pp iii (including Dedication dated Nov. 10, 1841, p. iii) + 192. BL and READING UNIV decorated cloth boards with gilt floral spray encircling *Godmother's Tales by Mrs. Hofland* on front, and floral motifs stamped in corners on front and back. Gilt decorated spine with title *Godmother's Tales*.

[BL, READING UNIV]

The Godmother's Tales also appeared in 'The Hofland Library' in the 1850s.

1843

62 THE KING'S SON: a romance of English history. Edited by Mrs. Hofland. Authoress of "Catherine the First; or, the Czarina" &c. &c. | Quotation from the Sermon of St. Paul's Cross. | In Three Volumes. Vol. I. London: Henry Colburn, Publisher, Great Marlborough Street. 1843.

18.7 × 12 cm. Printed by C. Whiting, Beaufort House, Strand, Pp (xiv) + 310 + 16pp advertising 'Mr. Colburn's New Publications,' dated 1843 - Vol. I; Pp 328 - Vol. II; Pp 302 - Vol. III. BL copy has three volumes rebound in one volume; SHEFFIELD has three volumes bound separately in modern library binding c.1926.

[BL, SHEFFIELD]

1844

63   EMILY'S REWARD: or, the holiday trip to Paris. By Mrs. Hofland, Author of "The Son of a Genius", "Ellen the Teacher", etc. | 1 line by Shakespeare. | London: Grant and Griffith, Successors to J. Harris, Corner of St. Paul's Churchyard. MDCCCXLIV

13.5 × 8.5 cm. Printed by S. and J. Bentley, Wilson, and Fley, Bangor House, Shoe Lane, London. Engraved frontispiece S. Williams. Pp xiii (including Preface dated Richmond, August 8, 1844, p viii) + 184 + pp 18 'Catalogue of Instructive and Amusing Works published by Grant and Griffith, successor to John Harris, Corner of St. Paul's Churchyard, London.' Blue cloth boards, on front stamped border decoration with gilt floral design in centre, on back similar border decorations but floral designs stamped only. Spine with raised bands, title in gilt *Emily's Reward/Mrs. Hofland*. SHEFFIELD rebound in modern library binding.

[BL, SHEFFIELD]

The Author's Preface (pp. (vii)-viii) refers to the 'great circulation given to her former works' and describes this book as one 'which both age and infirmity mark as her last.' It is dated Richmond, August 8, 1844.

64   HILDEBRAND: or, the days of Queen Elizabeth. An historical romance. By the author of "The King's Son." | 7 lines by Thomson | In three volumes. Vol. I. London: John Mortimer, Adelaide Street, Trafalgar Square. MDCCCXLIV.

18.5 × 10.6 cm. Printed by Henry Richards, Bridge-Street, Covent-Garden, London. Pp ii (including an advert for 'New Work, by the same author, preparing for publication, in 3 vols. 8vo. *The Old Temple*: an historical romance.') + 332 - vol. I; pp. ii (including the same advert) + 332 - Vol. II; pp ii (including the same advert) + 332 - Vol. III. SHEFFIELD COPY bound in three volumes in modern library binding c.1926.

[SHEFFIELD]

This historical novel, omitted by *CBEL*, is linked to Mrs Hofland by the authorship of *The King's Son*, and attributed to her by RAMSAY and *The English Catalogue of Books*, vol. I.

The half title verso carries an advertisement of a 'New Work by the Same Author. Preparing for Publication, in 3 vols., 8vo, *The Old Temple*: An Historical Romance, By the Author of "Hildebrand"', but no copy of this is known.

65   THE UNLOVED ONE; a domestic story. By Mrs. Hofland, Authoress of "Catherine I, Or the Czarina," &c. In Three Volumes. Vol. I. London: Henry Colburn, Publisher, Great Marlborough Street. 1844.

19.2 x 11.7 cm. Printed by Moyes and Barclay, Castle Street, Leicester Square, London. Pp 302 - Vol. I; Pp 307 - Vol. II; Pp 280 - Vol. III. BL and BOD have three volumes rebound as one in library binding, SHEFFIELD three volumes bound separately in modern library binding c.1926.

[BL, BOD, SHEFFIELD]

NUC records three American editions of this novel, all published in New York (in 1844, 1848 and 1867), while the book was also published in Routledge's 'Railway Library' series.

The Unloved One; *A Domestic Story*. By Mrs. Hofland, Authoress of Catherine I, or the Czarina, Etc. London: Routledge, Warne & Routledge .... 1860 'The Railway Library' series at Two Shillings.

1846

66   DANIEL DENNISON, AND THE CUMBERLAND STATESMAN. By the late Mrs. Hofland. In Three Volumes. Vol. I. London: Richard Bentley, New Burlington Street, 1846.

19.3 × 11.4 cm. Printed by Schulze and Co., 13, Poland Street, London. Pp 291 - Vol. I; Pp 288 - Vol. II; Pp 282 - Vol. III. BL and BOD have three volumes rebound as one in library binding, SHEFFIELD three volumes bound separately in modern library binding c.1926.

[BL, BOD, SHEFFIELD]

Daniel Dennison runs to volume II, p 113, and the *Cumberland Statesman* from vol II p. (117) to the end of vol III.

First published in 1846, it was republished by Bentley in 1848 (SHEFFIELD); and *NUC* cites editions in New York in 1847, 1866 and 1870 (?).

Editions

Most of Mrs Hofland's books were published, as we have seen, by John Harris, A.K. Newman or Longman and some were revised or enlarged when reprinted, the best examples being *The Son of a Genius* and *The Young Northern Traveller*. There was never, as far as we know, any intention that they should all be revised and re-issued in any kind of definitive collected edition.

After her death, however, there were several interesting reprints of Mrs Hofland's works. Griffiths & Farran, for example, republished four in 'The Favourite Library' between 1871 and 1883, and Nelson published no fewer than twelve of her books between 1866 and 1881.

The most remarkable edition of her works is, however, undoubtedly 'The Hofland Library', advertised by Arthur Hall, Virtue and Co. in the early 1850s. W. Jerdan's *Autobiography* (4 vols., London, 1852) contains an advertisement for it in vol. III, dated November 1, 1852, and the author's copy of *The Daughter-in-Law* has a similar advertisement dated January 1, 1853. The complete list of books published in this series, with First Class selling at 2s. 6d. and the Second Class at 1s. 6d. were numbered as follows:

The Hofland Library

First class
1   *Alfred Campbell; or Travels of a Young Pilgrim* (36)
2   *Decision; a Tale* (35)
3   *Energy* (57)
4   *Farewell Tales* (59)
5   *Fortitude* (55)
6   *Humility* (56)
7   *Integrity* (33)
8   *Moderation* (37)

9 *Patience* (34)
 10 *Reflection* (38)
 11 *Self-Denial* (41)
 12 *Young Cadet; or, Travels in Hindostan* (42)
 13 *Young Pilgrim; or, Alfred Campbell's Return* (40)

Second Class
  1 *Adelaide; or Massacre of St. Bartholomew* (31)
  2 *Affectionate Brothers* (20)
  3 *Alicia and her Aunt; or Think Before You Speak* (29)
  4 *Barbadoes Girl* (22)
  5 *Blind Farmer and his Children* (21)
  6 *Clergyman's Widow and her Young Family* (7)
  7 *Daughter-in-Law, her Father, and Family* (6)
  8 *Elizabeth and her Three Beggar-Boys* (51)
  9 *Godmother's Tales* (61)
 10 *Good Grandmother and her Offspring* (24)
 11 *Merchant's Widow and her Young Family* (17)
 12 *Rich Boys and Poor Boys; and other Tales* (52)
 13 *The Sisters, a Domestic Tale* (14)
 14 *Stolen Boy; an Indian Tale* (48)
 15 *William and his Uncle Ben* (39)
 16 *Young Northern Traveller* (15)
 17 *Young Crusoe; or, Shipwrecked Boy* (46)

Contributions to Annuals and Keepsakes

Mrs Hofland seems to have been a frequent contributor to many of the *Annuals* and *Keepsakes* which began to appear from 1823 onwards, often with very beautiful illustrations. Andrew Boyle identifies no fewer than 36 different contributions from her, including items for Ackermann's *Forget-Me-Not*, S.C. Hall's *The Amulet*, and Mrs S.C. Hall's *Juvenile Forget-Me-Not*.[1] In addition to these, 'Domestic Chit Chat' and 'A Visit to the Zoological Gardens' were published in *Spring Blossoms* (London, 1831), 'Frank and Will, The Little Chimney-Sweeps' in Montgomery's anthology *The Chimney-Sweeper's Friend* of 1824, and a poem and 'Conversations' in *The Northern Star* in 1818. Some of these contributions were then reprinted in single book form, as seems to have been the case with *The Stolen Boy*, and with some of the short stories which make up *Rich Boys and Poor Boys; and other Tales*.

---

[1] Andrew Boyle, *op. cit.* I, pp.129-30.

Attributions to Mrs Hofland

An Account of Fort-Montague, at Knaresborough

This four-page guide to a local Yorkshire beauty spot, printed by Hargrove and Sons at Knaresborough but undated, is part of the Hofland-Soane correspondence in the Soane Museum Library. It may be an anonymous pamphlet by Mrs Hofland, who had some dealings with Hargrove, but it is not mentioned by her in her letters of the time, and may simply be a souvenir of Soane's visit to Harrogate with Mrs Hofland in 1816. There is no evidence of her authorship.

The Abbess of Valtiera

RAMSAY attributes this work to Mrs Hofland (p xi), but Dorothy Blakey says it is by Agnes Lancaster[1]. The title-page of the BL copy clearly reads:

The Abbess of Valtiera; or the Sorrows of Falsehood.
A Romance.
In Four Volumes. By Agnes Lancaster.
London: Printed at the Minerva Press for A.K. Newman 1816

The Decision. A Novel By the Author of Caroline Ormsby, 3 vols., Longman, 1811.

This novel is attributed to Mrs Hofland by Block (op. cit. p 110) but by no one else. It has perhaps been confused with Mrs Hofland's tale, *Decision*, of 1824, (see 35 above) also published

---

[1] Dorothy Blakey, *The Minerva Press 1790-1820*, Oxford, 1939, p.252.

by Longman. BL records a copy of *Decision* in three volumes, and published by Longman in 1819, as by Anne Raikes Harding.

Roach Abbey: a Tale in Two Volumes: London, n.d.

Though attributed to Mrs Hofland and dated 1809 by RUSSELL, there are no references to it in other sources; the publishers (Ferguson and Co., Liverpool) were not used elsewhere; and the book is not mentioned by RAMSAY or in any correspondence.

Visits to the Parsonage

This pocket-sized volume, in which a Rector's children amuse themselves by reciting information about the British monarchy and Roman history, is attributed to Mrs Hofland by HARROGATE, and dated c.1810. As the title-page is missing, the book is not recorded elsewhere, and there is no supporting evidence, the attribution must be regarded as not yet proved.

A Week at Harrogate

This series of verse epistles, from BxxJxMxN BLxxDExHxxD to his friend SxMxN, was published by Hargrove and Sons of Harrogate in 1812. It is similar to Mrs Hofland's *A Season at Harrogate* (see 9 above), published by G. Wilson of Knaresborough and Harrogate, also in 1812, and is attributed to her by H & L, op. cit., IX, p364.

But, though we know Hargrove did ask Mrs Hofland for a verse guide to Harrogate, partly to puff his shop, she was unhappy about the payment, as her letters to Montgomery show (SHEFFIELD SLPS 1493), and her book was eventually published by Wilson with a signed Preface by Mrs Hofland, dated December 1, 1811, and with a note praising Mr Hofland's coloured prints of Bolton. *A Week at Harrogate*, which praises Hargrove's shop glowingly, makes no mention of either Mr or Mrs Hofland, and would surely have mentioned *The Season at Harrogate*, if Hargrove and the Hoflands were on good terms. It looks as if Hargrove did not offer Mrs Hofland enough money for the verse guide, or did not consider his shop praised enough, and so commissioned someone else to produce what he wanted. The North Yorkshire County Library, Harrogate, possesses a copy of *A Week at Harrogate* with the pencilled attribution to a local writer, David Lewis, author of many poems, chiefly of a comic and descriptive kind, so his authorship seems very likely.

William Tell

William Tell, or the Patriot of Switzerland, translated freely from the French of M. de Florian, and published by J. Harris and Son in 1823, seems to be attributed to Mrs Hofland by the *Monthly Literary Advertiser* for February 10, 1825, p10, and is so mentioned by MOON. But the block advertisement in the *Monthly Literary Advertiser*, though headed 'Mrs Hofland's Juvenile Works' and beginning with the names of eight books by her, concludes with *Minor Morals* by Charlotte Smith, *William Tell* by Florian, Tenth Edition, and *Keleth*, or *The Gatherer*. In other words, something seems to have gone wrong with the content of the Advertisement, and there seems no reason to attribute *William Tell* to Mrs Hofland other than that it appeared in a paragraph headed by her name but including two other works clearly not by her either. The Harris edition of 1823 is not the 'tenth edition'; the book is never mentioned by RAMSAY or other authorities; and though Mrs Hofland did have an interest in historical romances her authorship of this one seems unlikely stylistically.

York House, or Conversations in a ladies' school .... by Domina. London .... 1813.

This is attributed to Mrs Hofland by Block (op. cit., p111) on the evidence of a bookseller's catalogue. No copy of the book seems to be known now, and no one else makes this attribution.

Dates and locations of contemporary reviews

British Critic

La Féte de la Rose, XXXIV, June 1809
Little Dramas for Young People, XXXVI, July 1810
A Season at Harrogate, XXXIX, June 1812
Says She to her Neighbour, What?, XL, July 1812

Critical Review

Says She to her Neighbour, What? II, 4, October 1812
Ellen the Teacher, I, 4, April 1815
A Father as he Should be, II, I, July 1815
The Son of a Genius, IV, 6, December 1816

Gentleman's Magazine

The History of an Officer's Widow, LXXIX, May 1809
The Son of a Genius, LXXXIV, October 1814
Theodore, or the Crusaders, LXXXIV XCII, February 1822
Decision, XCVI, December 1826

Monthly Review

The History of an Officer's Widow, LXI, January 1810
Says She to her Neighbour, What?, LXIX, September 1812
Ellen the Teacher, LXXX, May 1816
The Blind Farmer, LXXX, July 1816

New Edinburgh Review

Tales of the Manor, IV, 7, January 1823

New Monthly Magazine

Richmond and its Scenery, November 1831
The Captives in India, August 1834
The Czarina, October 1842
The King's Son, May 1843

Quarterly Review

'Children's Books', LXXIV, June 1844

A select bibliography

Adburgham, Alison	*Women in Print; Writing Women and Women's Magazines from the Restoration to the Accession of Victoria*, London, 1972.
Altick, R.D.	*The English Common Reader. A Social History of the Mass Reading Public 1800-1900*, Chicago, 1967.
Avery, G.	*Childhood's Pattern*, London, 1975.
————	*Nineteenth Century Children*, London, 1965.
Bald, Marjorie A.	*Women Writers of the Nineteenth Century*, Cambridge, 1923.

Basch, Françoise — *Relative Creatures: Victorian Women in Society and the Novel 1837-1867*, trs. A. Rudolph, London, 1974.

Blakey, Dorothy — *The Minerva Press 1790-1820*, Oxford, 1939.

Block, Andrew — *The English Novel 1740-1850*, revised edition, London, 1963.

Boyle, Andrew — *An Index to the Annuals*, Vol. I, *The Authors (1820-1850)*, Worcester, 1967.

Bratton, J.S. — *The Impact of Victorian Children's Fiction*, London, 1981.

Butler, Marilyn — *Maria Edgeworth: A Literary biography*, Oxford, 1972.

Catalogue Générale des livres imprimés de la Bibliotèque Nationale, vol. 72, Paris, 1920.

The Catalogue of the Osborne Collection of Children's Books, prepared by Judith St John, 2 vols, Toronto, 1958-75.

Colby, Richard A. — *Fiction with a Purpose*, Indiana, 1967.

Colby, Vineta — *Yesterday's Women: Domestic Realism in the English Novel*, Princeton, 1974.

Cox, E. and Chandler, J.E. — *The House of Longman 1724-1924*, London, 1925.

Cruse, Amy	*The Englishman and his Books in the Early Nineteenth Century*, New York, 1956.
Cutt, M. Nancy	*Mrs. Sherwood and her Books for Children*, Oxford, 1974.
————	*Ministering Angels: A Study of nineteenth-century evangelical writing for children*, Wormley, 1979.
Dalziel, Margaret	*Popular Fiction 100 Years Ago*, London, 1957
Darton, F.J. Harvey	*Children's Books in England*, 3rd edition, revised by Brian Alderson, Cambridge, 1982.
Edgeworth, Maria	*The Life and Letters of Maria Edgeworth*, edited by Augustus J.C. Hare, 2 vols, London, 1894.

The English Catalogue of Books, 1801-1889, 5 vols, New York 1963.

Field, Mrs E.M.	*The Child and His Book*, London, 1891.
Fielding, Sarah,	*The Governess, or, Little Female Acadamy*, introduction by Jill E. Grey, Oxford, 1968.
Gettman, R.A.	*A Victorian Publisher: A study of the Bentley Papers*, Cambridge, 1960.

Goldie, Alexander	'The Moral or Educational Tale of the Early Nineteenth Century', thesis for PhD degree \ University of Edinburgh, 1951.
Grylls, David	*Guardians and Angels: Parents and Children in Nineteenth-Century Literature*, London, 1978.
Halkett, S. and Laing, J.	*Dictionary of Anonymous and Pseudonymous English Literature*, new and enlarged edition, by J. Kennedy and W. A. Smith, 9 vols, London, 1926-62.
Hall, S.C.	*A Book of Memories of Great Men and Women of the Age from Personal Acquaintance*, 3rd edition, London, n.d.
Hofland, T.C.	*The British Angler's Manual*, new edition, revised by E. Jesse, London, 1848.
———	*Fourteen Views of the Mansion and Garden Seats of White-Knights from Pictures and Drawings made on the Spot* by T.C. Hofland, London, n.d.
———	*Specimens of Garden Decorations and Oriental Scenery, Appropriate to Pleasure Grounds, selected from White-Knights* .... engraved from Drawings by T.C. Hofland, London, 1846.

Holland, J. and Everett, J.	*Memoirs of the Life and Writings of James Montgomery*, including selections from his remains in prose and verse, and conversations on various subjects, 7 vols, London, 1854-1856.
Hopkins, Mary A.	*Hannah More and her Circle*, New York, 1947.
Houghton, W.E.	*The Victorian Frame of Mind, 1830-1870.* Yale, 1957.
Houghton, W.E. (editor)	*The Wellesley Index to Victorian Periodicals 1824-1900*, 3 vols, Toronto, 1966-79.
Jacobus, Mary (editor)	*Women Writing and Writing about Women*, London, 1979.
James, Louis	*Fiction for the Working Man 1830-1850. A study of the literature produced for the working classes in early Victorian urban England*, second impression, Harmondsworth, 1974
Jolly, Rosemary	'Fiction for Children 1790-1840', thesis for M.A. degree, Birmingham University, 1968.

Juvenile Review, London 1817.

Leader, R.E.	*Reminiscences of Old Sheffield*, second

edition, Sheffield, 1876.

Sheffield in the Eighteenth Century, second edition, Sheffield, 1905.

L'Estrange, Revd A.G. (editor)   *The Friendships of M. R. Mitford*, 2 vols, London, 1882.

McKillop, A.D.   'Charlotte Smith's Letters', *Huntingdon Library Quarterly*, vol 15, 1952.

Moers, Ellen   *Literary Women*, London, 1977.

Moon, Marjorie   *Benjamin Tabart's Juvenile Library: A bibliography of books for children published, written, edited and sold by Mr Tabart, 1801-1820*, Winchester, 1990.

John Harris's Books for Youth 1801-1843, with supplement published in 1983, Winchester, 1987.

More, Hannah   *The Works*, new edition, 11 vols, London, 1830.

The National Union Catalogue Pre-1956 Imprints, Vol 250, London, 1973.

Neff, Wanda F.   *Victorian Working Women*, London, 1929.

Neil, Stephen   *Anglicanism*, Harmondsworth, 1958.

Peterson, M. Jeanne	'The Victorian Governess: Status Incongruence in Family and Society', *Suffer and Be Still: Women in the Victorian Age*, edited by Martha Vicinus, Indiana, 1973.
Ramsay, Thomas	*The Life and Literary Remains of Barbara Hofland*, London, 1849.
Russell, June	*Bibliography of Barbara Hofland*, Sheffield City Library, 1950.
Salmon, Edward	*Juvenile Literature as It Is*, London, 1888.
Salway, Lance	*A Peculiar Gift: Nineteenth Century Writings on Books for Children*, London, 1976.
Sangster, Paul	*Pity My Simplicity*, London, 1963.
Sherwood, Mary Martha	*The Life and Times of Mrs Sherwood*, edited by F. J. Harvey Darton, London, 1910.
Soames, Mary	*The Profligate Duke: George Spencer-Churchill, Fifth Duke of Marlborough, and his Duchess*, London, 1987.
Sutherland, J.A.	*Victorian Novelists and Publishers*, London, 1976.
Tawney, R.H.	*Religion and the Rise of Capitalism*,

London. 1964.

Terry, J.A.   'Attitudes Towards Pleasure and Instruction in Discussion of Children's Literature, 1780-1850', thesis for M.Phil. degree, University of London, 1969.

Thomson, Patricia   *The Victorian Heroine*, Oxford, 1957.

Tompkins, J.M.S.   *The Popular Novel in England 1770-1800*, London, 1932.

Walton, Mary   *Sheffield: its Story and its Achievements*, fourth edition, Sheffield, 1968.

Watson, George, et al (editors)   *The New Cambridge Bibliography of English Literature*, 5 vols, Cambridge, 1974-77.

Watt, Robert   *Bibliotheca Britannica*, 4 vols, Edinburgh, 1824.

Weber, Max   *The Protestant Ethic and the Spirit of Capitalism*, tr Talcott Parsons, second edition, London 1976.

Wigley, J.   'James Montgomery and the 'Sheffield Iris', 1792-1835', *Transactions of the Hunter Society*, vol 10, 1971-77, pp 172-81.

Wood, J.C.   'Thomas Christopher Hofland Painter and Angler 1777-1843', *The*

Connoisseur, July, 1977

Yarde, D.M. *The Life and Works of Sarah Trimmer*, Hounslow, 1972.

Yonge, C.M. 'Children's Literature of the Last Century', *Macmillan's Magazine*, London, August, 1869.

——— *What Books to Lend and What to Give*, London, 1887.

Index of artists, engravers and printers

Bacon, F., engraver, 88
Barnard, G., artist, 85
Bentham and Ray, Sheffield printers, 68
Bentley, Samuel, London printer, 87
Bentley, S. and J., Wilson and Fley, London printers, 93
Bentley, S. and R., printers, 73, 78, 79, 87
Bryer, H., London printer, 65, 67, 71, 73
Burney, E., artist, 58, 64, 77, 82, 83, 85

Childs, J. and R., Bungay printers, 75, 76, 77, 79
Corbould, H., artist, 75
Cox and Bayliss, London printers, 76

Darling & Son, London printers, 90, 91, 92
Darling, J., London printer, 58, 62, 64, 65, 66, 67, 68, 72, 77, 80, 82, 83, 85, 86, 89
Davison, T., London printer, 57, 61
Dean and Munday, printers, 81

Engleheart, T.S., engraver, 76, 79
Evans, W. (?), engraver, 81

Finden, E., engraver, 75
Fussell, artist, 81

Halne Brothers, printers, 91
Hall, Frederick, Oxford printer, 88
Harding, J.D., artist, 85
Hargrove and Sons, Yorkshire printers, 57
Hayter, J., artist, 75
Heath, engraver, 64

116 Barbara Hofland

Hemstead, R., London printer, 61
Hetz (?), artist, 62

Lane, Darling and Co., London printers, 59, 60, 64
Levey, Robson and Franklyn, London printers, 87, 88

Metz, engraver, 64
Mitchell, engraver, 77
Montgomery, J., Shefield printer, 56
Moyes, J., London printer, 61
Moyes and Barclay, London printers, 94

Raw, J., Ipswich printer, 63
Richter, H., artist, 88

Schulze and Co., London printers, 95
Shoberl Jun., Frederic, printer, 84

Shoberl Jun., J., London printer, 92
Smith, Frederick, artist and engraver, 85
Spottiswoode, A. and R., London printers, 70, 74, 80, 83
Springsguth, S., engraver, 58, 64, 77, 82, 83, 85, 86, 89, 91
Stothard, T., RA, artist, 74

Thomson & Hall, engravers, 80

Walker, engraver, 62
Walker, J.G., engraver, 74, 75
Whiting, C., London printer, 93
Whittingham, C., printer, 85
Williams, J., artist, 86
Williams, S., artist, 90, 91, 92, 93
Wilson, G., Yorkshire printer, 60
Wilson, W., London printer, 57, 69
Woodfall, G., London printer, 69
Wright, J.M., artist, 76, 77, 79, 89

Index of Barbara Hofland's works

The number in parenthesis is the number of the work in the chronological listing of Mrs. Hofland's works, and the number in bold indicates the page numbers of the main bibliographical descriptions.

Adelaide; or, the Intrepid Daughter (No. 31): 31, **73**, 97
Affectionate Brothers, The (No. 20): 32, **67**, 97
Africa Described (No. 43): 31, 40, **80**
Alfred Campbell, The Young Pilgrim (No. 36): 59, **76**, 96
Alicia and her Aunt; or, Think before you Speak (No. 29): 7, 34, **72**, 97

Barbadoes Girl, The See *Matilda; or the Barbadoes Girl* (No. 22)
Beatrice (No. 47): 40, **83**

Blind Farmer and his Children, The (No. 21): 7, 18, 22, 26, 29, 39, 44, **67-68**, 97, 103
Captives in India, The, and A Widow and a Will (No. 53): 26, **87**, 104
Cumberland Statesman, The (No. 66): 26, **94-95**
Czarina, The (No. 60): **91-92**, 104

Daniel Dennison and the Cumberland Statesman (No. 66): 26, **94-95**
Daughter-in-Law, The (No. 6): 4, 23, 26, **58-59**, 97
Daughter of a Genius, The, (No. 32): 5, 23, 29, 42, **73-74**

117

Decision (No. 35): 16, 26, 34, 35, 40, **75-76**, 96, 99-100, 103
Description of the House and Museum on the North Side of Lincoln's Inn Fields, the residence of Sir John Soane (No. 54): **87-88**
Descriptive Account of the Mansion and Gardens of White-Knights, A (No. 25): **69-70**

Elizabeth and her Three Beggar Boys (No. 51): 7, 32, 34, 71, **85-86**, 97
Ellen, the Teacher (No. 16): 7, 22, 30, 31, 34, 39, 41-42, 44, **65**, 103
Emily's Reward; or, The Holiday Trip to Paris (No. 63): 6, 39, **93**
Energy (No. 57): **89-90**, 96

Farewell Tales (No. 59): **91**, 96
Father as he Should Be, A (No. 19): 38, **66-67**, 103
Fête de la Rose, La (No. 2): 38, 44, **56**, 103
Fortitude (No. 55): **88-89**, 96
Funeral, The, A monody to the memory of the Princess Charlotte (No. 23): **68-69**

Godmother's Tales, The (No. 61): 25, 39, **92**, 97
Good Grandmother, and her Offspring, The (No. 24): 32, 34, **69**, 97

Hildebrand: or the days of Queen Elizabeth (No. 64): **93-94**
History of a Clergyman's Widow and her Young Family, The (No. 7): 32, 34, 47, **59**, 97

History of an Officer's Widow, The (No. 3): 3, 7, 32, 38, 39, 42, **57**, 103
Humility (No. 56): **89**, 96

Illustrated Alphabet, The (No. 58): **90-91**
Integrity (No. 33): 16, 40, 41, 44, **74**, 96
Iwanowna; or, the Maid of Moscow (No. 11): **61-62**

Katherine (No. 44): **80-81**
King's Son, The (No. 62): 24, **93**, 104

Letter of an Englishwoman, A (No. 26): **70**
Little Dramas for Young People (No. 4): 38, 40, **57**, 103

Matilda, or the Barbadoes Girl (No. 22): **68**, 97
Merchant's Widow and her Family, The (No. 17): 25, 26, 29, 33, 36, **65-66**, 97
Moderation (No. 37): 16, 23, 31, 40, 47, **76-77**, 96

Panorama of Europe, The; or a new game of Geography (No. 12): 31, **62**
Patience (No. 34): 40, **75**, 97
Patience and Perseverance; or, the Modern Griselda (No. 13): 16, 38, **62-63**
Poems (No. 1): 2, 38, **56**
Poetical Illustrations of the Various Scenes Represented in Mr Linton's "Sketches" in Italy (No. 49): **84-85**

Reflection (No. 38): 16, 23, 40, **77**, 97
Rich Boys and Poor Boys; and other tales (No. 52): 17, **86-87**, 97, 98
Richmond, and its Surrounding Scenery (No. 50): **85**, 104

Says She to her Neighbour, What? (No. 8): 5, 26, 38, 42, 44, **59-60**, 103
Season at Harrogate, A (No. 9): 38, 40, **60**, 100, 103
Self Denial (No. 41): 16, 28, 36, 40, 47, **78-79**, 97
Sisters, The (No. 14): 23, 40, **63**, 97
Son of a Genius, The (No. 10): 4, 6, 7, 18, 21, 23, 29, 30, 32, 33, 39, 41, 42, 46, 47, **60-61**, 103
Stolen Boy, The (No. 48): 24, 41, **83-84**, 97, 98

Tales in Verse (No. 5): 38, **57-58**
Tales of Clairmont Castle (No. 45a): **81**
Tales of Clairmont Castle (No. 45b): **81-82**
Tales of the Manor (No. 30): 40, **72-73**, 103

Tales of the Priory (No. 27): 40, **70-71**
Theodore, or the Crusaders (No. 28): 5, 42, **71-72**, 103

Unloved One, The (No. 65): 29, **94**

Visit to London, A, or Emily and her Friends (No. 18): 4, **66**

Widow and a Will, A (No. 53): 26, **87**
William and his Uncle Ben (No. 39): 5, **77-78**, 97

Young Cadet, The; or Henry Delamere's Voyage to India (No. 42): **79-80**, 97
Young Crusoe, The (No. 46): 24, 42, **82-83**, 97
Young Northern Traveller, The (No. 15): **63-64**, 97
Young Pilgrim, The, or Alfred Campbell's Return to the East (No. 40): **78**, 97

General index

Abbess of Valtiera, The, by Agnes Lancaster, 99
Aberdeen University Library, (ABER), 52, 83
Ackermann, Rudolph, *Forget-Me-Not*, 41, 98; *Ackermann's Juvenile Forget-me-not*, 86
Adburgham, Alison, *Women in Print: Writing Women and Women's Magazines*. 47
Addison, 68
Adventures of Ariston, The, by an Eton Boy, 84
Aikin, Dr., 43
Alcott, Louisa, *Little Women*, 46
Alderson, Brian, 8; revision of *Children's Books in England* by F.J. Harvey Darton, 52
Altick, R.D., 38; *The English Common Reader*, 47
Amulet, The, edited by S.C. Hall, 98
Annuals, 6, 41, 50, 98
Aristotle, 22

Assemblée, La Belle, 5
Athenaeum, The, 82
Austen, Jane, 16, 21, 23, 32; *Mansfield Park*, 46
Author's Copy, (AC), 52, 56, 59, 63, 69, 78, 79, 82, 86
Avery, Gillian, 20, 26
Ayrton, Margaretta, 91

Bacon, 68
Baines, 60
Baudry's 'European' and 'Juvenile Library', 61
Beattie, 67
Bell, D., Mr. and Mrs., (BELL), 52, 61, 67, 68, 72, 79, 89, 90
Bentley, Richard, 41, 87, 94-95
Bertrand, A., 61
Bibliography of Barbara Hofland, (RUSSELL), by June Russell, 54, 71, 100
Bibliotecha Britannica by Robert Watt, 66

Blakey, Dorothy, 38; *The Minerva Press 1790-1820*, 47, 66, 99
Blandford, Marquis of (later 4th Duke of Marlborough), 4-5, 69-70
Block, Andrew, (BLOCK), *The English Novel 1740-1850*, 49, 52, 99, 102
Boarding School Recollections, 73
Bodleian Library, The, (BOD), 52, 59, 60, 61, 65, 66, 71, 72, 74, 76, 77, 81, 83, 87, 90, 92, 94, 95
Bolton, Arthur T., 88
Book of Memories of Great Men and Women of the Age, A, by S.C. Hall, 9
Bott, Dr. M., 8
Boyle, Andrew, *An Index to the Annuals*, 47, 84, 98
British Critic, The, 44, 47, 103
British Library, The, (BL), 52, 56, 57, 58, 59, 60, 62, 63, 64, 65, 66, 67, 68, 69, 71, 72, 73, 74, 75, 76, 77, 78, 79, 81, 82, 83, 84, 85, 86, 87, 88, 89, 91, 92, 93, 94, 95, 100
Brontës, the, 1; *Jane Eyre*, 7, 31, 46; Rev. Patrick Brontë, 31
Brown, See Longman
Bubethas, Madame (later Babet), 59
Burnett, Frances Hodgson, 46
Butler, Marilyn, 8; *Maria Edgworth*, 47
Butts, Dennis, 9; See also Author's Copy, (AC)

Cameron, Lucy, 1
Canary Bird, The, by Alicia Catherine Mant, 69
Caroline, Queen, 70
Carroll, Lewis, 46

Catalogue of the Bibliothèque Nationale (BIB), 41, 47, 52, 61, 64, 65, 66, 68, 74, 80, 84
Catalogue of the Osborne Collection, The, (OSB), 53, 56, 81
Cervantes, 72
Chandler, J.E., See Cox, E.
Charlotte, Princess, 68
Charlotte, Queen, 4, 58, 66
Chase and Nicoll, 42
Chaucer, 81
Cheap Repository Tracts, by Hannah More, 15, 20
Chorley, Henry, *Letters of Mary Russell Mitford*, 26, 47
Colburn, Henry, 41, 87, 92, 93, 94
Colby, R.A., 45; *Fiction with a Purpose*, 48
Congreve, 57
Cowper, 57, 62
Cox, E. and Chandler, J.E., *The House of Longman 1724-1924*, 47
Crabbe, 77, 88, 89
Critical Review, 43, 103
Crosby, B. and R., 61
Crosby, R. See Crosby, B.
Cutt, M. Nancy, *Mrs. Sherwood and her Books for Children*, 25

Darton, F.J. Harvey, *Children's Books in England*, 36, 52
Day, Thomas, 14, 17; *Sandford and Merton*, 12-13
Decision, by Anne Raikes Harding, 100
Defoe, *Moll Flanders*, 21
Dickens, 1, 21; *David Copperfield*, 46; *Oliver Twist*, 7, 46
Domina, 102

Indices 123

Duke of Marlborough, The, See the Marquess of Blandford
Duchess of Northumberland, The, 85
Duke of Sussex, The, 88

Eastlake, Lady, 18: 'Children's Books', 43
Ecclesiastes, 90
Edinburgh Review, 43
Edgeworth, Maria, 1, 4, 12, 13, 14, 16, 17, 41, 47; *The Parent's Assistant*, 13; *Moral Tales*, 13; *Harry and Lucy*, 13; 'The Purple Jar', 13
Edgeworth, R.L., 12, 17, 18, 38, 39, 47
Edwards, 60
Edwards, Dr. J.A., 8
Elizabeth, Princess, 66
English Catalogue of Printed Books, The, (EC), 52, 63, 65, 66, 67, 71, 74, 76, 77, 78, 80, 83, 86, 89, 94
English Common Reader, The, by R.D. Altick, 47
English Novel 1740-1850, The, by Andrew Block, 49, 52, 99, 102
Eton Boy, An, 84
Evangelical Magazine, The, 15
Exile, The, 69

Fabulous Histories Designed for the Instruction of Children, by Mrs. Sarah Trimmer, 14
Fairchild Family, The, by Mrs. Sherwood, 15
Family Magazine, The, 14
Ferguson and Co., 100
Few Weeks at Clairmont Castle, A, by Miss Pearson, 82
Fielding, 21

Finden's Tableaux, 41
Florian, *William Tell, or the Patriot of Switzerland*, 101
Forget-Me-Not, 41, 98
Foster, Dr. Shirley, 8

Gales, A. and E., 57
Gales, Miss, 60
Gardiner, Alfonzo, 18, 43, 83
Gaskell, Mrs., 1
Genlis, Mme. de, 43
Gentleman's Magazine, The, 3, 43, 58, 70, 92, 103
George IV, 70
Gittings, Dr. Robert, 8
Goubaud, 67
Grant and Griffiths, 39, 61, 74, 93
Green, See Longman
Griffiths and Farran, 42, 61, 65, 72, 74, 96
Guardian of Education, The, 43
Gumuchian & Cie, (GUMUCHIAN), *Les Livres de L'Enfance du XVe au XIXe Siècle*, 53, 63, 78, 82, 83

Halkett, Samuel, and Laing, John, (H & L), *Dictionary of Anonymous and Pseudonymous Literature*, ed. J. Kennedy and W.A. Smith, 49, 53, 81, 100
Hall, Arthur, 63
Hall, Arthur, Virtue & Co., 42, 59, 77, 86, 96
Hall, S.C., *A Book of Memories of Great Men and Women of the Age*, 9; *The Amulet*, 98
Hall, S.C., Mrs., *Juvenile Forget-me-Not*, 98
Harding, Anna Raikes, 100

Hare, Augustus, J.C., *The Life and Letters of Maria Edgeworth*, 47
Hargrove and Sons, 57, 100-101
Harris, John, 3, 38, 39, 57, 61, 65, 67, 68, 71, 72, 73, 74, 76, 78, 79, 93, 96, 101; See also Marjorie Moon, *John Harris's Books for Children*
Harrogate, North Yorkshire Country Library, (HARROGATE), 53, 60, 100, 101
Harry and Lucy, by Maria Edgeworth, 13
Harvard University Library, 58
Haydon, Benjamin, 4
Heywood, John, 83
History of the Robins, The, by Mrs. Sarah Trimmer, 14
Hofland, Barbara, Mrs: born Barbara Wreaks, 1770, 2; education and early verse, 2; marriage to Thomas Hoole, 2; widowed and publishes *Poems*, 2; runs boarding-school in Harrogate, 3; first children's story, 3; marries Thomas Hofland and moves to London, 3; unhappy marriage, 4; works for Marquis of Blandford, 4-5; continues writing, 5; buries son Frederick, 6; death of husband, 6; own illness and death, 6; Mrs Hofland the writer, 11-25; literary career and earnings, 37-46; her views on Religion, the Family, Education and Work, 14, 20-21, 27-36, *passim*.
'Hofland Library, The', 42, 59, 63, 64, 67, 68, 69, 72, 73, 74, 75, 76, 77, 78, 79, 80, 83, 84, 86, 87, 89, 90, 92, 96-97

Hofland, Thomas Christopher, marries Barbara Hoole, 3; exhibits at Royal Academy, 3; moves to London, 3; wins art prize, 4; works for Marquis of Blandford, 4-5; art exhibition fails, 5; poor health, 3, 4, 6; illegitimate son, 4; visits Italy, but dies on return, 6
Hofland, Thomas Richard, Hofland's illegitimate son, 4
Hoole, Frederick, born, 2; at Moravian school, 3; falls ill and dies, 6
Hoole, Thomas, Barbara Hofland's first husband, 2
House of Longman 1724-1924, The, by E. Cox and J.E. Chandler, 47
Hunsley and Thomas, 60
Hunter, R., 69
Hurst, See Longman

Index to the Annuals, An, by Andrew Boyle, 47, 84, 98
Inglis, Dr. Fred, 8
Instructive Tales, by Mrs. Trimmer, 14
Iris, The, 2, 37, 56

Jane Eyre, by Charlotte Brontë, 7, 31, 46
Jerdan, W., 96
Job, 74
Johnson, Dr., 65; *The Rambler*, 66
Johnson, Mr., 69
Juvenile Forget-me-not, by Mrs. S.C. Hall, 86, 98
Juvenile Review, The, 43
Juvenile Souvenir, The, 84

Keepsakes, 98

Keleth, or The Gatherer, 101
Kennedy, J. and Smith, W., See Halkett, Samuel and Laing, John

Laing, John, See Halkett, Samuel
Lancaster, Agnes, 99
Lane, William, 38
Langdale, 60
Lant, Sophia, 62
L'Estrange, Rev. A.G., *The Life of Mary Russell Mitford*, 36, 70
Lewis, David, 101
Library of the Fine Arts, The, 84
Life of Mary Russell Mitford, The, by Rev. A.G. L'Estrange, 36, 70
Life and Literary Remains of Barbara Hofland, by Thomas Ramsay, (RAMSAY), 7-8, 42, 47, 49, 53, 66, 81, 94, 99, 100, 101
Lilly Library, (LILLY), Indiana University, U.S.A., 53, 58
Linton, W., 84, 85
Literary Gazette, The, 43, 44, 48, 84
Little Women, by Louisa Alcott, 46
Longman Archive, The, 8, 40, 47, 53, 56, 57, 60, 63, 71, 73, 74, 75, 77, 79, 80, 83
Longman (various combinations of Longman, Hurst, Rees, Orme, Brown and Green), 38, 39, 40, 56, 57, 60, 63, 70, 71, 80, 83, 96, 100

Macmillan Magazine, 43
Mansfield Park, 46
Mant, Alicia, Catherine, *The Canary Bird*, 69
Marlborough, Duke of, 5, 69-70
Marquis of Blandford, The, (later Duke of Marlborough), 4-5, 69-70

McKillop, A.D., 'Charlotte Smith's Letters', 47
Metropolitan, The, 84
Minerva Press, 38, 39, 59, 60, 62, 63, 65, 66, 67, 68, 99; See also Dorothy Blakey, *The Minerva Press 1790-1820*
Minor Morals, by Charlotte Smith, 101
Mitford, Mary, 4, 19, 26, 36, 41, 47, 70
Moers, Ellen, 19
Molesworth, Mrs., 25
Moll Flanders, by Defoe, 21
Montgomery, James, 2, 6, 37, 38, 56, 61, 100; *The Chimney-Sweeper's Friend*, 98
Monthly, The, 43
Monthly Literary Advertiser, The, 101
Monthly Review, The, 43, 44, 47, 48, 103
Montolieu, Mme. la Baronne de, 61
Moon, Marjorie, 8, 39; *John Harris's Books for Youth 1801-1843*, (MOON), 47, 53, 57, 61, 65, 68, 71, 72, 73, 74, 76, 78, 80, 101
Moral Tales, by Maria Edgeworth, 13
More, Hannah, 17, 18, 70; *Cheap Repository Tracts*, 15, 20; *The Shepherd of Salisbury Plain*, 18
Morning Post, The, 84
Mortimer, John, 93

National Art Library, Victoria and Albert Museum, 53, 68

126 Barbara Hofland

National Union Catalogue, (NUC), 42, 47, 53, 56, 57, 58, 59, 60, 61, 62, 63, 65, 66, 67, 68, 69, 71, 72, 73, 74, 75, 76, 77, 78, 79, 80, 82, 83, 84, 86, 87, 90, 92, 94, 95
Nelson and Sons, 42, 59, 63, 66, 67, 68, 69, 72, 74, 76, 77, 78, 83, 86, 89, 96
Nesbit, Mrs., 25; *The Railway Children*, 46
Newbery, John, 11
New Cambridge Bibliography of English Literature, The, (CBEL), edited by George Watson, 8, 49, 52, 59, 62, 63, 64, 66, 67, 68, 69, 71, 72, 74, 75, 77, 78, 79, 80, 81, 82, 87, 89, 94
Newbery, Elizabeth, 39; Newberry (sic) 57
New Edinburgh Review, 103
Newman, A.K., 38, 39, 41, 42, 58, 59, 60, 62, 63, 64, 65, 66, 67, 68, 69, 72, 73, 75, 76, 77, 78, 79, 80, 81, 82, 83, 84, 85, 86, 88, 89, 90, 91, 92, 96, 99
New Monthly, The, 43, 84, 104
New Year's Gift, 86
Nicholls, I., See Nicholls, L. & I.
Nicholls, L. & I., 60
Northern Star, The, 69, 98
Numbers, 78

Oliver Twist, by Charles Dickens, 7
Orme, See Longman

Parent's Assistant, The, by Maria Edgeworth, 13
Pearson, Miss, *A Few Weeks at Clairmont Castle*, 82
Pocket Books, 41, 50

Popular Novel in England 1770-1800, The, by J.M.S. Tompkins, 25
Postles, Dr. D., 8
Proverbs, 61, 69, 86
'Purple Jar, The', by Maria Edgeworth, 13

Quarterly Review, The, 43, 104
Quayle, Eric, 8, 53, 60

Rambler, The, 66
Ramsay, Thomas, *The Life and Literary Remains of Barbara Hofland*, (RAMSAY), 7-8, 42, 47, 49, 53, 66, 81, 94, 99, 100, 101
Reading Public Library, (READING LIB), 53, 70
Reading University Library, (READING UNIV), 53, 57, 60, 63, 68, 69, 74, 79, 80, 82, 83, 86, 90, 91, 92
Rees, See Longman
Renier Collection of Children's Books, The, (RENIER), 54, 66, 69, 74, 75, 76, 77, 78, 79, 83, 84
Richardson, 16
Roach Abbey, 100
Robinson, 60
Robinson, G., and Robinson, S., 61
Robinson, S. See Robinson, G.
Rousseau, 12, 14
Routledge's 'The Railway Library', 94
Russell, June (RUSSELL), *Bibliography of Barbara Hofland*, 54, 71, 86, 100

St. Paul, 75, 76; *Ephesians*, 89
St. Peter, 89

Sandford and Merton, by Thomas Day, 12-13
Sangster, Paul, *Pity My Simplicity*, 25
Second Maiden's Tragedy, The, 80, 81
Sermon of St. Paul's Cross, The, 92
Shakespeare, 71, 77, 79, 83, 92, 93
Sheffield City Library, (SHEFFIELD), 54, 56, 57, 59, 60, 62, 63, 64, 65, 66, 67, 68, 69, 71, 72, 74, 75, 76, 77, 78, 79, 81, 83, 84, 85, 86, 88, 89, 91, 92, 93, 94, 95, 100
Shepherd of Salisbury Plain, The, by Hannah More, 18
Sherwood, Mrs., 1, 17; *The Fairchild Family*, 15; *Susan Gray*, 15; M. Nancy Cutt, *Mrs. Sherwood and her Books for Children*, 25
Smith, Charlotte, 41, 47; *Minor Morals*, 101
Soane, John, 4, 24; Sir John Soane Museum Library, (SOANE), 54, 65, 70, 85, 87, 88
Spring Blossoms, 98
Stevenson, R.L., 46
Story of Clarissa, The, 69
Susan Gray, by Mrs. Sherwood, 15

Tabart & Co., 57
Thomas, See Hunsley and Thomas
Thomson, Patricia, 33; *The Victorian Heroine*, 36
Thomson (poet), 62, 67, 69, 93
Todd, 60
Todd and Sons, 58
Tompkins, J.M.S., 16; *The Popular Novel in England 1770-1800*, 25

Trimmer, Mrs. Sarah, *Fabulous Histories Designed for the Instruction of Children* and *The Robins*, 14; *Instructive Tales*, 14; *The Guardian of Education*, 43

Virtue & Co., See Hall, Arthur
Visits to the Parsonage, 100

Walters, Margaret, 8
Watson, George, See *The New Cambridge Bibliography of English Literature, (CBEL)*
Watt, Robert, *Bibliotheca Brittanica*, 66
Week at Harrogate, A, 100, 101
Whiteknights, 5, 69-70
William Tell, or the Patriot of Switzerland, by Florian, 101
Wilson and Son, 57
Wilson, G., 100, 101
Wilson, R., 60
Withers, George, 81
Wollstonecraft, Mary, 17
Wolstenholme, 60
Women in Print: Writing Women and Women's Magazines by Alison Adburgham, 47
Wotton, Henry, 81
Wright, 60

Yonge, Charlotte, 'Children's Literature', 43; *The Daisy Chain*, 46
York House, by Domina, 102

Zimmerman, 63